ANNUA

UK POLITICS

Sarra Jenkins
Nick Gallop

HODDER
EDUCATION
AN HACHETTE UK COMPANY

Hodder Education, an Hachette UK company, Blenheim Court, George Street, Banbury, Oxfordshire OX16 5BH

Orders

Bookpoint Ltd, 130 Park Drive, Milton Park, Abingdon, Oxfordshire OX14 4SE
tel: 01235 827827
fax: 01235 400401
e-mail: education@bookpoint.co.uk

Lines are open 9.00 a.m.–5.00 p.m., Monday to Saturday, with a 24-hour message answering service. You can also order through the Hodder Education website: www.hoddereducation.co.uk

ISBN 978-1-5104-4764-6

First printed 2019

Impression number 5 4 3 2 1

Year 2022 2021 2020 2019

Typeset by Integra Software Services Pvt. Ltd., Pondicherry, India

Cover photo: IRStone/Adobe Stock

Printed by CPI Group (UK) Ltd, Croydon, CR0 4YY

Hachette UK's policy is to use papers that are natural, renewable and recyclable products and made from wood grown in well-managed forests and other controlled sources. The logging and manufacturing processes are expected to conform to the environmental regulations of the country of origin.

MIX
Paper from
responsible sources
FSC™ C104740
FSC
www.fsc.org

Contents

Contents

Chapter 1

Democracy and elections: first-past-the-post and the impact on UK politics

Exam success

The examination specifications focus on far more than just the workings of first-past-the-post (FPTP). They look specifically at the advantages and disadvantages of this system, both alone and compared to the multiple systems now at use in the UK. Moreover, they look at the impact of these systems. The best candidates will understand this impact can be assessed in a range of ways, looking at the type of government formed, the effect on the people or the choices they have, or on the legitimacy of the entire political system. Whilst there was not a general election in 2018, top answers will be able to use the political situations of this year to illustrate the impacts of the system. This includes two by-elections, the first use of the recall petition, the government report on the redrawing of constituency boundaries and the breaking of the Cambridge Analytica scandal.

Edexcel	UK Politics 3.1	The advantages and disadvantages of first-past-the-post
	UK Politics 3.3	The impact of the electoral system on the government or the type of government appointed
AQA	3.1.2.2	Debates around the performance of first-past-the-post
		The advantages and disadvantages of this system

Context

FPTP has long been used for UK general elections. The division of the UK into roughly equally sized constituencies allows for the election of a local MP in each area. Long-touted for its ability to return a strong, single-party government, the last three elections have challenged this traditional wisdom. 2010 saw a coalition government formed, 2015 a majority government but only just, and 2017 a minority government propped up by a confidence and supply agreement between the Conservatives and Northern Ireland's Democratic Unionist Party (DUP).

In addition, the changing voting patterns of these elections has further called into question the role of this system, especially during an era when other systems have been tried and tested within the UK. Ironically, whilst FPTP failed to produce a majority in 2010, the 2011 election in Scotland produced a single-party government despite using a proportional electoral system.

Table 1.1 show the election results in the UK from 1997 to 2017. Note the inconsistencies between the percentage of the vote gained, and the number of seats gained, and variance in the average vote needed per seats between parties.

Table 1.1 Election results in the UK 1997–2017

	Labour		Conservative		Liberal Democrat		UKIP	
	Votes (%)	Seats	Votes (%)	Seats	Votes (%)	Seats	Votes (%)	Seats
1997	43.2	418	30.7	165	16.8	46	0.3	0
2001	40.7	412	31.7	166	18.3	52	1.5	0
2005	35.2	356	32.4	198	22.0	62	2.2	0
2010	29.0	258	36.1	306	23.0	57	3.1	0
2015	30.4	232	36.9	331	7.9	8	12.6	1
2017	40.0	262	42.4	317	7.4	12	1.8	0

Throughout 2018, Theresa May was embattled due to the general election result; a minority government with a divided party and an empowered House of Lords. The return of the Boundary Commission's consultation on UK constituencies in 2018 also threw up allegations similar to 'gerrymandering' in the USA. Equally, the Cambridge Analytica scandal that broke over the use of Facebook data in the 2016 presidential election exposed flaws in FPTP in the UK.

The Boundary Commission report

In 2016, the independent Boundary Commission undertook a boundary review of the 650 UK constituencies. It looked to reduce the number of MPs from 650 to 600, agreed by Parliament in 2011, and would have happened earlier but lacked the support of the Liberal Democrats during the Coalition. The review was completed and reported to the government in September 2018. If approved by Parliament, it will be in place for the 2022 general election.

What did the report propose?

The law requires that periodically boundaries of constituencies are reviewed to reflect moving and growing populations. The final report, following public consultation, suggested:

- 501 English constituencies; a loss of 32
- 53 Scottish constituencies; a loss of 6
- 29 Welsh constituencies; a loss of 11
- 17 Northern Irish constituencies; a loss of 1

This would also result in constituencies that were more equal in terms of population with each constituency having a population of between 71,031 and

78,507 (except for the Isle of Wight which must have two constituencies regardless of population). Just 15% of UK constituencies would remain unchanged.

What difference would the reforms make?

The reforms should reduce the disparity over the number of votes that are currently needed to win a seat that results from the difference in constituency population.

The reforms were not well received by MPs. Conservatives have argued that current boundaries are a disadvantage to them, and the recommended proposals are likely to remedy this somewhat. However, it would also threaten the seats of notable Conservative figures such as Boris Johnson and David Davis. Johnson's currently heavily Conservative constituency would be altered to include a more heavily Labour-leaning area (around Northolt), potentially challenging his 5,000 vote majority, whilst Davis' constituency would disappear entirely.

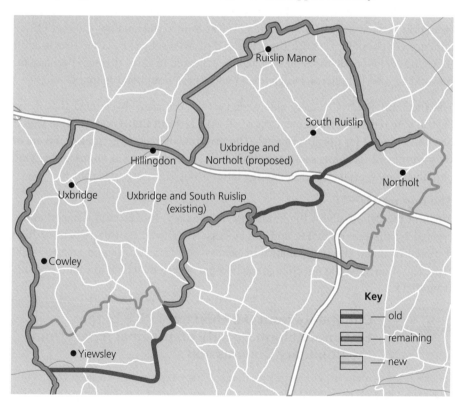

Figure 1.1 Boris Johnson's current and proposed constituency boundaries

For the Conservatives, the newly proposed boundaries would have seen them win an overall majority of 16 seats in 2017, rather than the minority government they found themselves with. Nonetheless, Conservative backbenchers who would see their seat or majority threatened by the review were deeply angry, so much so that it was suggested that May might not try to implement the changes immediately, delaying a vote on the proposals until after Christmas.

The Labour Party was equally outraged, calling the review an 'undemocratic power grab'. The review would move the boundaries of Jeremy Corbyn's constituency such that it would effectively merge with Diane Abbott's seat. A good number of high-profile Labour MPs would find themselves in a challenging situation having their seat abolished or merged, among them Gareth Snell, Owen Smith and Rachel Reeves.

Given the advantage these boundaries would give to the Conservatives, Labour has accused them of 'gerrymandering', an American term used to describe the drawing of constituency boundaries to gain a political advantage. A Cabinet Office statement commented that the reports were prepared independently and impartially, therefore this is not gerrymandering, but this has done little to quell anger on both sides.

It is more broadly controversial in the wake of Brexit. With big issues such as this being decided by Parliament, the reduction in the number of MPs could lead to a reduction in scrutiny of the government. Cat Smith, the shadow Cabinet Office minister commented: '... with the workload of MPs set to rise after Brexit, with thousands of pieces of important legislation expected to come through Parliament, it would be utterly ludicrous to go ahead with these boundary changes.'

The Electoral Reform Society also added to the criticism. It claimed that if the payroll vote remained the same, 23% of all MPs (45% of Conservative MPs) would be bound to vote for the government. The 'payroll vote' are appointed members of the government – cabinet secretaries, ministers, junior ministers, whips and private parliamentary secretaries, although the latter is not actually a paid role.

The impact of FPTP

Much of the debate about the boundary reforms revolves around issues that are created by the use of FPTP, and not necessarily solved by this reform. Whilst it aimed to make the mathematics of general elections fairer and ensure equal representation, it would not change the two-party system, which ultimately results from FPTP.

Box 1.1 **Comments from the chief executive of the Electoral Reform Society on the final report from the Boundary Commission**

Cutting the number of MPs with Brexit around the corner would be like a company laying off its staff having just secured a major new contract. Backbench scrutiny will be needed more than ever after we leave, making this cut hugely irresponsible.

And claims that the proposed boundaries would 'equalise' the voting system are a red herring. 22 million votes were wasted at last year's general election — they made no contribution to the result in each seat. That's 68% of the total votes cast. That is the effect of Westminster's first-past-the-post voting system — not lines on a map.

Meanwhile one in five voters felt forced to 'hold their nose' and opt for a second or third choice party to keep out someone else. That's the real inequality in our system — and it needs tackling by giving voters the fair, proportional voting system we need.

Source: www.electoral-reform.org

The first recall petition

In 2015, the Recall of MPs Act was passed allowing for constituents to force their MP into a by-election if they can collect the signatures of 10% of that constituency.

In July 2018, North Antrim MP Ian Paisley was suspended from the House of Commons for 30 days for failing to declare holidays he had taken that were paid for by the Sri Lankan government. His constituents followed this suspension by using the Recall of MPs Act for the first time since it became a law to try to force him into a by-election. After 6 weeks, however, the petition closed. At this point, they had only gained signatures of 9.4% of his constituents, a result that Paisley described as 'a miracle'.

The influence of FPTP

Whilst the use of the recall petition failed, the role of FPTP is nonetheless notable. Firstly, Paisley represents a very safe seat. In 2017, he gained 58.9% of the votes. This was 42.6% more than the second-biggest party in this constituency, Sinn Fein. Holding such a safe seat made the recall petition unlikely to be successful on two fronts. First, the constituency was substantially dominated by his supporters, making the chances of reaching the 10% of signatures necessary more difficult. Second, had he faced a recall election, the chances of him retaining his seat was incredibly high and therefore may have suppressed interest in the petition. This law that is designed to ensure the accountability of MPs is seriously undermined by the use of FPTP.

The Cambridge Analytica scandal

The Cambridge Analytica scandal revolved around the collection of personal data from Facebook without users' knowledge. This data was then being used for political purposes in the 2016 presidential election and even in the Brexit referendum. The data collected created profiles about voters which was used to make targeted adverts online to try to sway their vote.

Why is this relevant to FPTP?

According to the *Guardian*, this scandal is crucial as it exposes flaws that can be particularly exploited in FPTP. The Conservative Party could currently possess a majority if, in 2017, 'just 533 people had voted differently in just nine constituencies'. Given that spending in marginal seats is an average of 37.5% higher than in safe seats, it is easy to see how data such as that provided by Cambridge Analytica could help to better target these seats. However, this would add yet more importance to swing seats, and further reduce interest in safe seats, effectively disenfranchising great swathes of the UK population.

A key reason for this flaw is FPTP itself. It allows small groups of voters to have undue importance. If a proportional system were used, it would equalise voter value and therefore reduce the democratic dangers such as those posed by companies like Cambridge Analytica. Whilst FPTP is maintained, the likelihood of other companies trying to do the same thing remains high.

2018 by-elections

There were two by-elections held in 2018 — in West Tyrone and Lewisham East — both triggered by the resignation of MPs who held those seats. Notably, both seats were exceptionally safe seats in 2017, with 67.9% of the Lewisham East vote going to Labour MP Heidi Alexander and 50.7% of the West Tyrone vote going to Sinn Fein's Barry McElduff. It was not surprising then that both parties retained their seats in these by-elections.

Why is this relevant to FPTP?

These results serve to underline the key problem with FPTP — the inequality of voter value. In these two seats, the majority taken in 2017 made it unlikely that the result would go any other way in 2018. This depresses turnout — just 55% in West Tyrone and 33% in Lewisham East, which serves to undermine the legitimacy of those elected. That these are safe seats is a direct result of the use of FPTP.

Comparison: the UK and US electoral systems

The UK and US both use FPTP for their national elections. The results of this are unsurprisingly similar.

- Both the USA and UK have a two-party system despite growing third party presence. UKIP gained around 4 million votes in 2015 whilst third parties in the USA gained nearly 8 million votes in 2016 (nearly four times as many as in 2012, perhaps as a result of the 2016 candidates being Donald Trump and Hillary Clinton). Despite this, the success of third parties seems to be lower than ever and only the Conservatives, Labour in the UK, and the Democrats and Republicans in the USA have a realistic chance of forming a government.
- Both countries have been recently accused of 'gerrymandering', in the UK through the Boundary Commission's proposals, whilst in the USA there has been a spate of cases regarding this practice referred to the Supreme Court. This continues to ensure the dominance of two parties and the distortion of voter value.
- Both the USA and UK have been victims of the Cambridge Analytica scandal. Similarly, both countries see disproportionate amounts of money spent by candidates campaigning in swing seats.

Edexcel	Comparative Politics 6.2.9	The different nature of the party systems
AQA	3.2.2.4	Comparisons of elections and electoral systems used in the UK and USA
		Comparisons of the two party system and how they operate in the UK and the USA

Summary

Whilst there was no general election in 2018, events ensured that FPTP came under continued scrutiny. In a digital media age and with a growth of political interest following the events such as the Scottish independence referendum, Brexit and the election of Jeremy Corbyn as Labour leader, it is questionable whether FPTP is reflective of the needs of the UK in the twenty-first century. This is especially true given that the Conservative vote increased in 2017 yet the number of seats they gained decreased.

Further debates include:

- whether FPTP still lives up to the strengths it is purported to have traditionally given to the UK
- if it is necessary to review the use of FPTP for UK-wide elections, especially given the success of proportional systems elsewhere in the UK
- the necessity of exploring other voting methods to increase turnout, such as e-voting
- the effectiveness of representation on constituency level, especially with the prospect of boundary reforms now far more realistic
- the role and significance of third parties in FPTP in recent elections

Further reading and research

- Read 'First past the post leaves UK elections uniquely vulnerable to data hijack' by Brian Eno, 6 April 2018, **www.theguardian.com**.
- Read Channel 4 FactCheck 'How would parliament look after proportional representation?', Martin Williams, 24 August 2017, (**www.channel4.com/ news/factcheck**).
- Find out more about the impact that the Boundary Commission's review will have on your constituency by entering your postcode on **www.bce2018.org.uk**.
- Aiming for an A? Read 'David Cameron: why keeping first past the post is vital for democracy', 30 April 2011, **www. telegraph.co.uk**. How many of these arguments are weaker or stronger today given the last two election results and other national circumstances?

Chapter 2

Rights in the UK: 2018 and the conflict between individual and collective rights

Exam success

The Edexcel and AQA specifications have focused sections on debates and tensions over civil rights in the UK and the extent of the conflict between individual and collective rights. Also within the Edexcel specification is the requirement to study the work of two contemporary civil liberty pressure groups. Students aiming for the highest level in their examination responses should be able to analyse contemporary examples of rights issues, evaluate recent instances of tension between individual and collective rights and demonstrate breadth and depth of knowledge in discussing recent activities and campaigns of civil liberties groups.

Edexcel	UK Politics 1.4	Debates on the extent, limits and tensions within the UK's rights-based culture, including consideration of how individual and collective right may conflict
AQA	3.1.1.1	Debates about the extent of rights in the UK

Context

Conflict and tension between individual and collective rights, liberty and security, are permanent features of modern liberal democratic states in which groups are free to challenge legislation or regulation that is perceived to be excessively restrictive or discriminatory. Table 2.1 provides a snapshot of several of the higher profile and ongoing campaigns in 2018, two of which are studied in further depth later in this chapter.

The seemingly disparate issues listed in Table 2.1 are in fact characterised by many of the same questions and debates. First, which rights should be considered fundamental and universal, and which should be subject to the discretion of the state? Second, when it comes to choices over civil liberties, who should decide their extent — judges, elected politicians or people? Third, and with a focus on the A-level specification, where should the balance lie between upholding individual rights and protecting citizens and the state from potentially deadly threats? In this third question lies the conflict between individual and collective rights.

Table 2.1 Examples of ongoing civil rights campaigns in 2018

Campaign area	Explanation
Protecting soldiers	Seeking to protect soldiers' rights whilst serving at home or abroad, from issues such as unsafe equipment and miscarriages of justice.
Counter-terror measures	Resisting government measures to infringe civil liberties, such as retaining biometric data, censorship and 'suspicionless' detention.
The Snoopers' Charter (The Investigatory Powers Act)	200,000 people have signed a petition to stop the so-called Snoopers' Charter which, according to civil liberty groups, represents an excessive intrusion into private lives.
Data sharing between public services and immigration enforcement	Campaigns to stop government departments (especially the Home Office) obtaining information from public services (e.g. schools and hospitals) to target vulnerable groups.
LGBT awareness	Supporting LGBT equality and raising awareness of discrimination affecting the LGBT community, challenging prejudice and campaigning for fairness and equality in the workplace.
Public Space Protection Orders (PSPOs)	The criminalisation of non-criminal behaviour within specified areas. Many PSPOs are deemed to target vulnerable groups.
Indefinite detention	The UK detains a high number of vulnerable people each year — asylum seekers, survivors of torture and trafficking — with no limits on how long they can be held.
Facial recognition software	Law enforcement agencies scanning faces at public gatherings and comparing them against 'hidden' databases. There is very little regulation of this kind of activity.

Box 2.1   Civil rights and human rights

Civil rights are granted to citizens within a state. They usually relate to social and political freedoms — such as equality and privacy — and define relationships between citizens and the state, such as the right to vote, to free speech and to a fair trial.

Human rights are not seen as being at the discretion of the state; instead they are said to be 'inalienable' or fundamental to every human being. Examples include the right to life and freedom from torture.

Contemporary case studies in 2018: the work of two civil liberty pressure groups in the UK

38 Degrees

Founded in 2009, 38 Degrees takes its name from 'the angle at which snowflakes come together to form an avalanche' and is the UK's largest community-based pressure group, which claims to have around 2 million members. 38 Degrees targets its efforts by directly and regularly appealing to its broad membership for campaign priorities. The front page of its website asks: 'What would you like to change in the UK?' and surveys 50,000 randomly selected members to vote for campaign priorities each week.

38 Degrees campaign successes in 2018 include:

- **Plastic pollution (March 2018):** environmental charity Surfers Against Sewage started the 'bottle deposits' petition on the 38 Degrees website. With 329,616 signatures, the petition and subsequent campaign were prominent in the national news and seen as instrumental in Environment Secretary Michael Gove's decision to bring back 'bottle deposits'.
- **Oil drilling in Surrey (September 2018):** planned oil drilling near Leith Hill, a popular beauty spot in Surrey, was dropped after a petition-led campaign by 38 Degrees that highlighted risks to water pollution and other adverse consequence for local citizens.

Recent criticisms of 38 Degrees include:

- Several MPs have highlighted the '**nuisance**' nature of 38 Degrees online tactics, drawing particular attention to the high frequency of spam-like e-mails sent to elected representatives and officials relating to its campaigns, and the creation of multiple 'clone e-mails' from its website.
- Other MPs have drawn attention to some 38 Degrees campaigns as 'alarmist', 'scare-mongering' or '**irresponsible**', in particular those relating to highly emotive issues such as reforms to local public services and local healthcare provision.

The Fawcett Society

The Fawcett Society is an organisation that campaigns for women's rights, its origins dating back over 150 years to Millicent Fawcett's lifelong peaceful campaign for women's suffrage. As the group states, its primary focus is on 'women's representation in politics and public life; pay, pensions and poverty; valuing caring work; and the treatment of women in the justice system' and, with many high-profile members and supporters, it is influential in raising the profile of women's issues and of gender inequality.

The Fawcett Society campaign successes in 2018 include:

- **Gender pay equality (April 2018):** as of April 2018, UK employers with over 250 employees are required to report their gender pay gaps (the average difference between the remuneration of men and women within the same company). The Fawcett society was particularly prominent in campaigning for transparency over gender pay parity and workplace inequality.
- **The All-Party Parliamentary Group (APPG) on Sex Equality (June 2018):** run by the Fawcett Society, the APPG on Sex Equality is a cross-party group of MPs and peers focusing primarily on gender equality. In June 2018 the group debated women's representation in politics, raising further awareness of levels of online abuse suffered by many female MPs, and of Westminster's inhospitable work environment.

Recent criticisms of the Fawcett Society include:

- The Fawcett Society's campaign to highlight the gender pay gap was criticised by business groups and the Statistics Authority for using **misleading data** that contrasted full-time male pay with part-time female pay to paint the bleakest picture. The group acknowledged their lack of transparency and has attempted to correct data and methodology.
- Some have criticised the Fawcett Society's demand for quotas to resolve gender disparities in various sectors of society. Whilst the highlighting of gender disparities has been universally welcomed – only 26% of university vice chancellors are female, as are just 6% of FTSE 100 chief executives – the group's demands for 'direct intervention' is seen as potentially **replacing one type of injustice with another**.

Collective rights over individual rights: public spaces protection orders (PSPOs)

Passed in 2014, the Anti-Social Behaviour, Crime and Policing Act consolidated and expanded law enforcement powers. Amongst several notable changes, the Act also set out the ability of councils to enforce public spaces protection orders (PSPOs). Unlike their much-derided forerunner anti-social behaviour orders (ASBOs), which focused on the behaviour of individuals, PSPOs enabled councils and other law-enforcement agencies to criminalise not normally criminal behaviour by outlawing certain activities within a defined space. Behaviours which can be tackled and controlled through PSPOs include:

- access to and rights over public land
- storage of household items, waste and wheelie bins
- consumption of alcohol in public spaces
- aggressive behaviours linked to begging, street selling or preaching

Table 2.2 Representative examples of PSPOs in recent years

Year	Council	Example
2015	Hackney	The council attempted to make rough sleeping a criminal offence within a designated area via a PSPO. The proposal was withdrawn after the council was served with an 80,000-signature petition.
2016	Southampton	The city council introduced PSPOs to control drinking and begging in the city centre. In December of that year, a tenant of the council became the first person to be prosecuted for a breach of the city's PSPO after being found begging in a car park.
2017	Durham	The county council introduced a dog control PSPO which will remain in force for 3 years and relates to the immediate removal of dog faeces and 'failing to place a dog on a lead when directed by an authorised officer'.
2018	Birmingham	By 2018, the city council had eight anti-social PSPOs in place which included those relating to drinking, loitering and off-road bikes, five PSPOs for dog control and six proposed PSPOs.

Growing controversy over the use of PSPOs required the Local Government Association (LGA) to issue guidance for councils on their use. In its 24-page document 'Public Spaces Protection Orders – Guidance for councils' issued in June 2018, the tension between individual and collective rights is well reflected in the use of PSPOs. As the LGA's guidance explains, whilst PSPOs have been used successfully 'in helping to make local areas safe places to live, visit and work and in tackling anti-social behaviour', there is recognition that some PSPOs have been implemented without adequate consultation, have targeted vulnerable individuals, especially the homeless or beggars, or have simply displaced problems from one area to another rather than providing a solution.

It is the escalation in the use of PSPOs that has concerned many civil liberties groups. Campaigners against PSPOs cite that:

- Towards the end of 2018 there were over 400 PSPOs in place in Wales alone.
- The range of some PSPOs is widely discriminatory. One PSPO in place in Dawlish makes it illegal to 'act in a manner as to cause annoyance … to any person'.
- They target the most vulnerable. Rough sleeping is not normally a lifestyle choice made voluntarily or by many people, but some councils have opted to use to PSPOs to criminalise it.

However, outlawing behaviours which, in the view of some councils, are likely to have a detrimental effect on the quality of life of those in the locality is often widely seen as sensible and effective. For many, it represents a far better situation than one which previously saw many local communities adversely affected by anti-social behaviour, and law enforcement agencies seemingly powerless to act against a small number of 'anti-social' individuals.

Individual rights over collective rights: data sharing and the protection of minorities

The General Data Protection Regulation (GDPR) Act came into force in May 2018 across the European Union with wide-ranging implications for the collection and processing of personal information. Whilst the GDPR Act is seen to encompass all organisations and individuals, civil liberties group the Migrants' Rights Network (MRN) highlighted and exposed an agreement in the form of a 'memorandum of understanding' that allowed data on patients, such as dates of birth and addresses, to be shared between the Home Office and the National Health Service for the purposes of immigration enforcement.

Even though the agreement pre-dated the GDPR Act, coming into force in January 2017, it was widely condemned by privacy and civil liberties campaigners and MPs amidst warnings that vulnerable individuals could be deterred from seeking medical treatment.

The MRN launched a legal challenge in the High Court in November 2017 asserting that revealing and sharing personal data in this way was in breach of the Data Protection Act (legislation that preceded the GDPR Act). Box 2.2 represents excerpts from the MRN's submissions to the High Court calling for a judicial review of the memorandum of understanding on the grounds of discrimination and breach of the right to privacy granted by the European Convention of Human Rights.

> **Box 2.2 The Migrants' Rights Network (MRN) High Court submissions (April 2018)**
>
> The MRN asserted in submissions to the High Court that the aim of the information sharing 'cannot reasonably be regarded as sufficiently important to justify the limitation of patients' fundamental rights' and constituted a breach of the confidential doctor–patient relationship.
>
> In addition, the MRN claimed that the interests of the wider community were also undermined by a limitation of patients' fundamental rights. The MRN argued that the overall effect would leave migrants 'too scared to access healthcare services they are entitled to', which could particularly affect victims of trafficking and abuse.

In April 2018, coordinated campaigns by several different health and civil rights groups in addition to the Migrants' Rights Network — such as Doctors of the World, the National AIDS Trust and Liberty — forced the government to acknowledge the NHS/Home Office agreement as an illegal breach of personal data under the then soon-to-be-enacted GDPR Act. The government agreed to dramatically curtail arrangements to share hospital data to trace undocumented people in a move that civil liberties groups regarded as a notable campaign success for the protection of individual rights.

Comparison: rights in the UK and USA

One of the most striking differences between politics in the UK and USA lies in the arena of civil rights. The Bill of Rights, the first 10 amendments to the US Constitution, unequivocally entrenches the basic rights of American citizens. In contrast, in the UK, there is no such document, and debates remain over the extent to which a British Bill of Rights could ever provide similar protections in the absence of a codified constitution. However, the constitutional clarity with which rights are protected in the USA has not diminished controversy. Two main contrasts between the UK and USA are as follows:

- Despite the US Bill of Rights, the federal structure of the USA and associated levels of state power have permitted stark differences in rights afforded to US citizens on the grounds of the colour of their skin. Such differences have cast a lengthy shadow over the USA's democratic history, in contrast to the relatively harmonious multicultural and multiethnic UK.
- Unlike the UK, the US Supreme Court is the foremost player in the protection of civil liberties in the USA. However, the highly politicised US Supreme Court has long been accused of finding and establishing civil liberties that, according to its critics, do not exist within the US Constitution. Whilst differences are historical, similarities may be more current. In the UK, the Human Rights Act (1998) and the creation of the UK Supreme Court (2009) have drawn judges into ever-greater conflict with other branches of government as their role as chief protector of civil liberties develops.

Edexcel	Comparative approaches 6.2.7	The effectiveness of the protection of rights in the UK and USA.
		The effectiveness of interest groups in the protection of civil rights in the USA and the UK
AQA	3.2.2.6	Similarities and differences regarding the protection of civil rights in the UK and the USA.
		Comparisons of methods, influence and effectiveness of civil rights campaigns in the UK and the USA

Both specifications require knowledge and understanding of the extent to which rational, cultural and structural approaches can be used to account for these similarities and differences.

Summary

Whilst a central focus of the debate over civil liberties is the extent to which there is a conflict between individual and collective rights, a further significant strand focuses on the trend for governments to expand their powers to the detriment of individual liberties and civil rights. Indeed, Labour, coalition and Conservative governments over the last two decades since 1997 have all had a mixed record on protecting civil and individual liberties. Ongoing debates over the 'extent' of rights in the UK have focused on:

- restrictions to basic rights, such as free speech and freedom of association, and the growth in accusations of 'authoritarianism' as an increasing number of regulations and laws are seen to curtail former freedoms
- detention, sometimes indefinite, of vulnerable individuals and groups such as asylum seekers and other undocumented migrants in the name of security
- restrictions in the rights to a trial by jury with many more crimes being tried at magistrates' level rather than in jury-based Crown Courts
- an ever-greater number of restrictive tools, including ASBOs, PSPOs and Community Protection Notices (CPNs), imposed by local councils and other law enforcement agencies

However, in many cases, arguments that governments are threatening civil liberties can be countered by arguments that, in doing so, they are protecting others. Closer examination reveals that framing the debate as one between state power and individual freedom is too simplistic. It is instead a complex multidimensional tension between different views of what constitutes 'liberty' and which, and whose, 'rights' should be protected.

Further reading and research

- For more on 38 Degrees visit **www.38degrees.org.uk**, and for more on the Fawcett Society visit **www.fawcettsociety.org.uk**. Also visit Liberty's website at **www.libertyhumanrights.org.uk**. Liberty is seen as the leading civil liberties campaign group in the UK, with many concurrent campaigns and some notable recent successes.
- Other prominent civil liberties groups worth researching for recent activities and successes are the LGBT campaign group Stonewall (**www.stonewall.org.uk**), the Migrants' Rights Network (**www.migrantsrights.org.uk**) mentioned in this chapter, and the Howard League for Penal Reform (**www.howardleague.org**) campaigning for prison reform and prisoners' rights.
- Read the Local Government Association's guidance: 'Getting Public Space Protection Orders right — what have we learnt so far' (5 June 2018) (**www.local.gov.uk**).
- Membership, debates and issues raised by the All-Party Parliamentary Group (APPG) on Sex Equality can be found on the Fawcett Society's website as it works as the APPG's secretariat.

Chapter 3

Political parties: did 2018 see a development or contraction in multiparty politics in the UK?

Exam success

The examination specifications focus on the 'development' of a multiparty system in the UK and look to evaluate the impact this has had on government. The best candidates will understand that given the pluralist nature of power in the UK, this could be evaluated beyond just Westminster. This could take in examples from the devolved bodies, mayoral constituencies and the European Parliament. Top answers will recognise and evaluate the political situation in 2018, which saw a notable change in party membership figures and the reasons for this, the suggestion of a 'new' UK political party to fill the vacant centre ground, and local elections in a number of English wards. All of this continues to be set against the ultimate creator of tensions within and between parties — Brexit.

Edexcel	UK Politics 2.4	The development of a multiparty system and its implication for government
AQA	3.1.2.3	Development towards a multiparty system in the UK and its impact on government and policy

Context

The UK has traditionally been dominated by two parties, with little in the way of bipartisanship between elections. This might have been the Tories competing with the Whigs in the seventeenth century, the Conservatives against the Liberals in the nineteenth century or the Labour Party against the Conservatives in the twentieth and twenty-first century. However, the decentralisation of power from Westminster since 1997, and the increase in the use of proportional electoral systems has seen a growth in the number of parties both competing and competing successfully in the UK. The SNP took outright control of the Scottish Parliament in 2014 and UKIP was the largest party in the UK's European elections of 2014.

Even within Westminster, under FPTP, which traditionally ensures two-party dominance, the moulds have been broken. In 2015, for the first time, a different party won in each country of the UK in the general election:

- England was won by the Conservatives
- Wales was won by Labour
- Scotland was won by SNP
- Northern Ireland was won by the Democratic Unionists

This was repeated in 2017. This suggests that a wider number of parties are being elected to Westminster, and to other elected bodies too, rather than the tradition two-party dominance. This should necessitate a move to multiparty politics in the UK with a greater variety of voices being heard in Parliament and devolved bodies. It is crucial to delineate between the meanings of multiparty politics however — in an electoral sense, it would refer to multiple parties having a realistic chance of forming government. Beyond this, it could also refer to the political importance of multiple parties within an elected body. In a non-election year, the latter definition becomes the focus.

Party membership in 2018

The election of 2017 saw a huge rise in the number of people voting for either the Conservatives or Labour. At a shared vote of 84% of those who voted, this was the highest total for the two parties since the 1970 election. However, constitutional scholar Professor Vernan Bogdanor claims that this should not be mistaken for the UK being regarded as merely a two-party system.

In 2018, the SNP became the second largest party in terms of membership. The Conservative Party was pushed into third place for the first time since the recorded data beginning in 1928. Similarly, despite its poor performance in the 2017 election, UKIP saw a surge in membership. In July, the number of people trying to join UKIP reportedly crashed its website, whilst in August its membership jumped by 15% increasing by 3,200 members.

Table 3.1 Party membership in the UK

	Membership in 2017	Membership in 2018
Labour	564,000	540,000
Conservative	149,000*	124,000
Liberal Democrats	97,000	99,000
SNP	118,000	125,000
UKIP	23,000	24,000
Green Party	42,000	39,000

* Based on 2013 figures, which was the last released data from the party

One of the key reasons behind these increases was Theresa May publishing the Chequers plan for Brexit. The unhappiness of those on the right at the perceived 'soft Brexit' fuelled the UKIP growth, whilst voters in Scotland, which had voted as a nation to remain, were equally dismayed at the plan for contrasting reasons.

> ### Box 3.1 Comments from MSP Derek Mackay, the SNP business convener (party chair)
>
> Over 7,000 people joined the SNP in just 5 days in June, propelling us ahead of a waning Tory party, which is at risk of imploding completely over Brexit.
>
> Like the extraordinary membership surge of 2014, joining the SNP has once again become not just a powerful symbol, but the best way to ensure Scotland's voice is heard.
>
> People were rightly outraged at Tory plans to remove powers from the Scottish Parliament, and that only 15 minutes were given over at Westminster to debate the impact of the EU Withdrawal Bill on devolution.

The major parties also saw changes in their membership in 2018. Factions within the Conservative and Labour parties both saw a 'surge' in membership. Labour's Momentum reached a total of 40,000 members in April, whilst the Conservatives saw a rise in membership following the release of the Chequers plan. It was suggested that this could be explained by those angered by the plan joining up to make their voices heard, leading to fears of a 'blue Momentum' pulling the party to the right. It certainly could be the case that people joined up to have a say in any leadership election given the headlines surrounding May's weakness as a prime minister.

Towards a multiparty UK?

The changes in membership certainly demonstrate the importance of more than simply the Conservative and Labour parties in UK politics. Even UKIP, which suffered hugely in the 2017 general election, can be seen to be having an impact — if nothing else, it is creating headlines and fuelling division in the Conservative Party. That the SNP are now the second largest party in the UK certainly suggests the growing influence of other UK parties. Nonetheless, party membership remains historically low as a percentage of the population.

A 'new' UK political party?

Headlines were made in the summer of 2018 with the suggestion that a new political party could be formed in the UK. Fuelled by the success of Macron's En Marche and the view that UK parties were not sufficiently different from one another, stories emerged of a possible new party that had gained £50 million of backing. A similar YouGov poll identified the top issues on which people did not feel that the main UK parties represented their views. Over a quarter of people in the poll held a belief that the justice system was not harsh enough, immigration should be tighter, government should regulate big business more or that Britain should intervene militarily in other countries, but they also felt that no main party represented these views.

Into this vacuum came the possibility of a new party that would fill the political centre ground for those who felt unrepresented. One option was that politicians disillusioned with current party politics, such a Chuka Umunna could form a new centrist party. At the same time the creation of United for Change by LoveFilm founder Simon Franks also became a possibility, with a scheduled launch in 2019. These parties would be trying to fill a perceived vacuum in the centre of UK politics drawing from both liberal and centre-right ideologies. United for Change was described as having 'an eclectic mix of policy ideas' that supported the NHS whilst cracking down on missed appointments and supported both social and pro-business policies. With two out of five voters saying they would vote for such a new party, huge significance was placed on these possibilities.

However, the UK political system proves a challenge for new political parties and United for Change seemed to stumble before it had even begun. In September 2018, its chief executive stepped aside to form his own splinter party, Twelve Together.

The headlines garnered by the possible new party do suggest that a change in UK party politics is underway. It certainly highlights the disillusionment felt by the general public with the current party set-up. However, the chances of such a party being able to break through in the UK political system remain low at national level.

Local elections in 2018

Local elections took place in 150 wards in England in 2018. These elections traditionally represent a more multiparty system of politics, with councils having members from multiple parties and some councils lacking an overall majority by one party. Political pundits often look to these elections as a barometer of the popularity of central government, but they reflect a far more multiparty picture than the national elections.

Table 3.2 Local elections results in 2018

	Councils controlled	Number of councillors elected (change)
Labour	74	2,350 (+79)
Conservative	46	1,332 (−35)
Liberal Democrat	9	536 (+75)
UKIP	0	39 (+8)
Green	0	3 (−123)

21 of the 150 councils (14%) returned results that meant no one party had control of the council. Beyond this, just 25 of the councils elected councillors from only the Conservative and Labour Party. In Cheltenham, the Labour Party returned not one councillor, whilst the same was true of the Conservative Party in Cambridge. In fact, of the 150 councils, three were controlled by just one party after the elections, whilst one had members of seven parties elected to it. Nonetheless, the actual change in the control of councils was limited – Liberal Democrats gained control in four councils, with Conservatives losing two and the number of councils with no overall control decreasing by two.

The fortune of the parties running in the local elections varied greatly inside and outside of London. In London, Labour made substantial gains whilst the Conservatives suffered heavy losses. Outside of the capital however, Labour's gains were far more modest, whilst the Conservatives did substantially better. The Liberal Democrats and Green Party made modest gains across the country whilst UKIP was decimated.

> ### Box 3.2 Karin Bottom (lecturer in British politics at the University of Birmingham) on the party nature of local elections
>
> Multiparty politics operates in English local councils and non-mainstream options continue to quietly grow. Though the predicted demise of UKIP will reduce small party representation, the Greens have more than doubled their candidacy.
>
> Arguing for an 'end to one-party-state councils' and a 'Green on every council', the party is articulating an explicitly 'bottom-up' approach and predicts success. Relatively new to local politics is the Women's Equality Party which will field 30 candidates and, if successful, bring a gendered narrative to the council chamber. So while Labour and the Conservatives might take all the headlines, there's an awful lot more going on around the country.

Towards a multiparty UK?

The local elections in 2018 show the vast importance of regional voting patterns, which support the notion that the UK is a multiparty system. They allowed for 108 councils to have representatives from between three and five parties on them, including a considerable number of independents. This is a pattern that is mirrored in the elections for the regional assemblies and even to some extent in the European elections. It demands that for the councils to function, parties must embody multiparty politics and work together.

Comparison: the UK and US party system

Given that both the USA and UK use FPTP, it is not surprising that both countries seem on the surface to have a two-party system. However, recent elections in both countries have seen a surge in third party support.

- Both the UK and USA have suffered from deepening divisions within their major parties. The Conservatives and Republicans remain divided over issues – Brexit and the policies of Donald Trump – whilst Labour and the Democrats are both suffering from a lack of a strong leader to rally and unite their parties.
- Within the UK devolved assemblies and councils and the US states, it is more apparent that two parties struggle to maintain dominance. In the USA, 31.3% of Americans live in a state that has no one party controlling the government; this amounts to 16 states spread across the USA. This is similar to the councils in the UK in which no one party has overall control.
- In both countries, despite a rise in support, third parties are ostensibly denied representation or power at national level due to the electoral and governmental infrastructure.

Edexcel	Comparative politics 6.2.9	The different nature of the party systems
		The degree of internal unity within parties
AQA	3.2.2.4	Comparisons of the two party systems and how they operate in the UK and the USA
		Explanations of why the USA has a two party system whilst the UK is moving towards a multiparty system

Summary

The UK system may appear to be dominated by two parties, but there are a multitude of factors to consider when looking at the role and impact of other parties. Whilst 2017 saw an increase in the vote share for the main parties, the backdrop of Brexit cannot be ignored as this became the defining issue of that election. Beyond national elections, it appears that voters are increasingly looking beyond the major parties.

Further debates include:

- whether the deepening factions in the major parties allow for broader representation of the voting public, or simply reduce the effectiveness of party representation
- if it is necessary to review the nature of UK elections in order to allow for the development of multiparty politics
- the necessity of exploring regional voting patterns and the reasons for this
- the effectiveness of representation of the voting public by the major UK parties
- the role and significance of third parties in the UK's representative democracy

Further reading and research

- Read Politico's article regarding a new party, 'Introducing Britain's new political party', 13 August 2018, **www.politico.eu**.
- Research and compare the full local elections results across the UK by finding 'Local council election result 2018 in full', **www.theguardian.com**. What do the differences show about regional voting patterns?
- Watch Professor Verdan Bogdanor's video reviewing the situation after the 2017 general election, 'From Two-Party to Multi-Party Politics', 15 May 2018, 6:00pm–7:00pm, **www.gresham.ac.uk**.
- Aiming for an A? Take a look at the Democratic Audit's SWOT analysis 'How democratic are the UK's political parties and party system', 22 August 2018, **democraticaudit.com**, regarding UK parties. Does this suggest the UK is moving towards or away from a multiparty system?

The Labour Party in 2018: did the left strike back?

Exam success

The examination specifications focus on the origins of political parties and the ideology underpinning their history. Through this lens, it is possible to track the development of party policies and identify how a party's ideology has evolved over time. The best candidates will understand that party ideology today is to some extent fluid rather than fixed, responding to changes in party leadership, public opinion and national events. Top answers will be able to draw on the experiences of the Labour Party in 2018. The left-wing group Momentum continued to gain membership and prominence supporting Jeremy Corbyn, a Labour leader more aligned to traditional Labour values. The party was also embroiled in a controversy over anti-Semitism, which challenged not only the moral beliefs of the party but also led to members being subjected to votes of no confidence and Corbyn's wreath-laying actions scrutinised. All of this continued whilst the Party was pressed for a position on the Brexit deal, and calls for a second referendum led to a shadow cabinet sacking.

Edexcel	UK Politics 2.2	The origins and historical development of the Labour Party, and how this has shaped their ideas and current policies on the economy, law and order, welfare and foreign policy
AQA	3.1.2.3	The origins, ideas and development of the Labour Party, and how this has helped to shape their current policies
		Party structures and functions of the Labour Party

Context

Formed in the early twentieth century, the Labour Party was founded on the principles of socialism to represent the urban working classes and fight for greater equality and wealth redistribution. The constitution adopted by the Party in 1918 included Clause IV, which pledged to 'secure for the workers by hand or by brain the full fruits of their industry' and sought for common ownership within the economy. The party moved away from this principle, rewriting Clause IV in 1995 under Tony Blair and winning three successive elections as New Labour by championing free market economics rather than socialism.

In 2015, Jeremy Corbyn was elected as the Labour Party leader. He is a committed socialist and notable rebel to New Labour, voting against the majority of his party in nearly 25% of votes between 2001 and 2010. In his campaign for leadership, he commented: 'I think we should talk about what the objectives of the party are, whether that's restoring Clause IV as it was originally written or it's a different one. But we shouldn't shy away from public participation, public investment in industry and public control of the railways.' His commitment to realigning the Labour Party with its ideological roots continued in 2018. Most visibly this was highlighted at the Labour Party conference of 2018 at which shadow chancellor John McDonnell reminded attendees:

> One hundred years ago in 1918 the Labour Party adopted Clause IV as part of our party's constitution. Let me remind you what it said: 'to secure for the workers, by hand or by brain, the full fruits of their industry'. I say the Clause IV principles are as relevant today as they were back then. Fair, democratic, collective solutions to the challenges of the modern economy.

Labour and Momentum

The left-wing, grassroots Labour Party movement Momentum made headlines in two key ways in 2018. First, the group's membership continued to grow. In the period between January and April 2018, membership of Momentum increased by 15%, and by then it had 40,000 members – this is more than the Green Party and UKIP. In January, it claimed to be growing by 1,000 members a month; by April it was 1,700 members a month. In fact, it launched a campaign in 2018 to overtake the membership of the Conservative Party by the next general election. This growth led its founder, Jon Lansman, to comment that 'Momentum is the new mainstream'.

Momentum is not, however, a party. All members of Momentum have to be a member of the Labour Party. Momentum is a grassroots movement of individuals who work on the ground, campaigning locally and nationally, providing back-up and support, developing digital tools and mobilising people to support the left wing of the Labour Party and Jeremy Corbyn.

Momentum's attempts to change the Party

The growth of Momentum is important because of the pressure that it can exert on the national Party. Just its consideration of consulting its members about supporting a second Brexit referendum made headlines – it was the first major group on the left wing to consider supporting this and represented a push for Labour to commit to a Brexit strategy.

Momentum was also instrumental in putting forward changes to the structural rules of the Labour Party at the party convention in Liverpool. It fought for MPs to have to automatically fight for reselection in their constituencies and to allow any other party member to stand against them. This would make it easier to remove sitting MPs and to replace them with candidates who were chosen by the members of the Party rather than the leadership. Whilst it lost this vote at the conference,

the fact that it was able to advance its demands to this level and get them voted upon demonstrates the power it currently holds within the Party.

It also demonstrated the growing tensions between Momentum and the unions that support the Labour Party. Momentum's suggestions would have given more power to members to select candidates, but the unions' objections resulted in the compromise that was passed. This tension was audibly evident, with shouts of 'shame' directed at the unions from the conference floor.

Box 4.1 Discipline within the Labour Party

Corbyn-sceptic groups Labour First and Progress have a joint slate, but left-wing Corbynite organisations have split after the Campaign for Labour Party Democracy (CLPD) announced its own slate independently of Momentum this morning. The set of candidates endorsed by CLPD is also backed by Jewish Voice for Labour (JVL), the Campaign for Nuclear Disarmament (LCND), Labour Briefing Co-Op and Labour Representation Committee (LRC).

This small paragraph is from an article ('The candidate slates for Labour's disciplinary NCC — in full', 11 October 2018 on **https://.labourlist/org**) regarding changes to the disciplinary procedures of the Labour Party that were made in 2018 following the anti-Semitism scandal. The number of members on the the National Constitution Committee (NCC), which deals with disciplinary issues, was increased from 11 to 25 members. Each of these factions wanted to nominate different people, their own 'slate', to these vacancies. It demonstrates just how many factions there are within the current Labour Party and hints at the tensions between the ideologies of these factions.

Equally, the founder of Momentum has a role on the NEC, Labour's National Executive Committee. This body decides the strategic direction for the Labour Party, so holding this role gives him, and by association the Momentum group, a foothold in the direction that the Labour Party will take. In 2018, Lansman even considered running for the post of Labour's general secretary in order to try to achieve changes to the structure of the party, making it more open and democratic. His decision brought him into direct conflict with trade unions such as Unite who was running its own candidate for this post supported by Shadow Chancellor John McDonnell. This exposed tensions even within one ideological wing of the party with both Unite and Momentum being key supporters of Jeremy Corbyn.

Box 4.2 Jon Lansman withdraws from the general secretary contest, March 2018

We must draw a clear line between our renewed and reinvigorated mass-membership party and previous eras of command and control — where the views of members and affiliates alike were too often ignored, party conference overruled and the NEC disrespected.

Momentum's impact on MPs and party ideology

One of the casualties of Momentum and the shift to the left in the Labour Party was the MP Frank Field. An MP of 39 years, he was one of only four Labour MPs to side with the prime minister's Brexit strategy. In fact, since the election in 2017, he has rebelled against his party in 27.6% of votes in which he has taken part. As a result, he was subjected to a vote of no confidence from his constituency members in July 2018 and was harshly criticised by Momentum leaders, saying that 'there is no room for Labour MPs who side with the reactionary Tory establishment'. In the same month, fellow Labour MP Kate Hoey was subjected to a similar vote in her Vauxhall constituency, and like Field she has rebelled in 33% of the votes in which she has taken part since June 2017. Both claimed to be acting in what they considered to be the best interests of the country, but the pressure under which they are being placed demonstrates the ideological shift towards the left of the Party in general.

> ### Box 4.3 Field and Hoey on their votes of no confidence
>
> Field said he acted for the 'millions of Labour voters — mainly in parts of the country that have long been neglected by the elites — who gave politicians a clear instruction to take the country out of the EU'.
>
> Hoey remarked that the result in the vote of no confidence was 'not a surprise — my local party activists are solid EU remainers. I will always put my country before my party and helping my constituents is a priority. After 29 years as an MP I am quite relaxed about the vote and it won't influence in any way how I vote in the future'.

The anti-Semitism controversy

There has been long-running controversy regarding the Labour Party and accusations of anti-Semitism within the party. In 2016, Ken Livingstone was suspended over claims of anti-Semitism, and in 2018 he resigned from the Party formally, whilst numerous actions of Jeremy Corbyn have been scrutinised and criticised for appearing to have Palestinian sympathies. The current Labour Party position on Israel and Palestine is to create a two-state solution, to reduce the human suffering of war and end — what they have viewed as — the West turning a blind eye to the military atrocities of Israel. This position is unusual in eastern politics, however, and left the Party open to claims of anti-Semitism.

The crisis highlighted further divisions within the Party. The confrontation between Hodge and Corbyn resulted initially in a disciplinary investigation into Hodge, although this was later abandoned. Former Labour leader and Prime Minister Tony Blair, speaking to the Holocaust Educational Trust, associated the anti-Semitism controversy that the party was embroiled in with the movement of the Party to the left: '… resurgence of anti-Semitism… does come back and in a way that brings out the demons of the far right and the far left.' He further claimed that the party was in denial over the issue.

Box 4.4 Timeline of the anti-Semitism controversy in 2018

March: Jewish leaders accuse Corbyn of 'siding with anti-Semites' for his apparent support of an anti-Semitic mural 6 years earlier.

May: Ken Livingstone resigns from the Labour Party following his suspension in 2016 in an anti-Semitic row.

July: Labour accepts the definition of anti-Semitism from the International Holocaust Remembrance Alliance (IHRA), but causes controversy by omitting the examples attached to their definition. This leads to a confrontation between Margaret Hodge MP and Jeremy Corbyn in which she called him a 'racist and anti-Semite'.

August: the three largest unions call on Labour to adopt the full IHRA definition of anti-Semitism.

September: Labour adopts the full IHRA definition of anti-Semitism. Noted MP Frank Fields resigns from the party whip saying that Labour risks becoming a 'force for anti-Semitism'.

The issue was further stoked when Field resigned from the party whip over the issue, echoing the sentiments of Blair. Field said: 'It saddens me to say that we are increasingly seen as a racist party' and that there was a culture of 'intolerance, nastiness and intimidation' within the party.

The anti-Semitism debate, whilst provoking controversy for the Labour Party, fuelled further concerns that Corbyn and his allies were looking for ways in which independently minded Labour MPs could be pushed out. This helps to explain the disciplinary action against Hodge amongst other MPs. Certainly, centrist Labour MPs have expressed their discontent with the Labour leadership's response, or lack thereof, to the anti-Semitism crisis.

Left at the party conference

In addition to the Clause IV references by John McDonnell, and the attempts to reform the democratic structures of the Labour Party, the party conference saw other allusions to the ideological movement within the Labour Party. The language used in a speech by MP Laura Smith echoed Old Labour ideology, with appeals to working-class action and calls for organisation and unification of the working classes.

Box 4.5 Laura Smith at the Labour Party Conference

Comrades, we must topple this cruel and callous Tory government as soon as we can. And if we can't get a general election we should organise with our brothers and sisters in the trade union [movement] to bring an end to this government with a general strike.

The language used by Smith, whilst criticised by deputy Labour leader Tom Watson, is reminiscent of the language of Old Labour.

Equally, the speeches of both Jeremy Corbyn and John McDonnell laid out a series of policies and ideological aims that are far more in keeping with a more left-wing political ideology:

- a promise to fight for democracy and social justice, and against poverty, inequality and discrimination, putting 'fairness and humanity' back into public services
- a call for change to the failing privatisation schemes of the UK, calling it a 'disaster zone', and pledging to bring water, energy, Royal Mail and rail into public ownership
- a description of austerity as 'social vandalism'
- giving the UK workforce a right to elect a third of board members in their companies, encouraging worker ownership of businesses, banning zero-hours contracts and setting a minimum wage of £10 an hour

These policies reflect a shift away from the policies advanced by Blair's New Labour to a more traditionally socialist ideology. McDonnell rounded off his speech saying: 'And you know… we'll be proud to call that future, socialism. Solidarity.'

Comparison: the left in the UK and the USA

Drawing comparisons between the Labour Party and parties in the USA is always a challenge, as the political landscape of the USA is considerably further to the right than that of the UK. That means there are few, even within the Democratic Party, who hold truly socialist views. However, there are comparisons that can be drawn:

- Both the Labour Party and Democratic Party have notable factions within them including those that represent the left or progressive wing of their party.
- Socialism in both countries is championed more by strong individuals than by parties themselves – Corbyn and McDonnell in the UK, and Sanders in the USA. Whilst Elizabeth Warren in the USA claims she is 'capitalist to my bones', she too is a well-known figure on the progressive wing of the party.
- The evolution of ideology shown within the Labour Party is reflected within the evolution of party and public polarisation regarding political allegiance.

Edexcel	Comparative Politics 6.2.9	The degree of internal unity within parties
		The policy profiles of the two main parties in each country
AQA	3.2.2.4	Degrees of internal unity within the parties in the UK and the USA
		Comparisons of party policies in the UK and the USA

Summary
Party ideologies do change over time. Parties are vehicles by which elections are fought and therefore the policies they choose will be those that they believe to be popular and will give them a chance to win an election. The movement of the Labour Party reflects the disillusionment of some of the British public with years of austerity coupled with poor management of the

Brexit negotiations by the Conservatives. Whether this ideology will be an election-winning strategy remains to be seen, but there certainly did seem to have been a resurgence of the ideological left within the Party in 2018.

Further debates include:

- whether the reforms to the democratic structures of the Labour Party need to be taken further
- whether it is necessary to reevaluate the ways in which MPs can be held accountable for their actions
- the extent of unity within the whole Labour Party under Corbyn
- the effectiveness of party leaders in shaping party ideology and unifying their parties
- the role and significance of grassroots movements and public opinion on party ideology and policy

Further reading and research

- Read 'Jeremy Corbyn speaking at Labour Party Conference today', 26 September 2018, https://labour.org.uk. Which elements can be identified as 'Old Labour' and 'New Labour'?
- Compare 'John McDonnell 's full speech to Labour Conference 2018' (24 September 2018, https://labour.org.uk) to that of Jeremy Corbyn — what differences can be identified?
- Find out more about the role of Corbyn as leader of the opposition. What problems does he face in this role? See 'Jeremy Corbyn is failing Britain with inept opposition', 6 August 2018, www.ft.com.
- Aiming for an A? Research some of the factions named in Box 4.1 and identify the conflicts that exist between these groups.

Chapter 5

Pressure groups: continuity and change in methods and influence

Exam success

The examination specifications focus on exactly how pressure groups are able to exert influence in the UK. This does not specify influence over Parliament and therefore their methods utilising a range of access points could be explored. The best candidates will focus on the differences between pressure groups, explaining how they choose the methods that they do and why they are more or less likely to be successful. This crucially means looking at a variety of pressure group action, rather than just the direct action that tends to make the headlines. Top answers will evaluate the changing nature of pressure group action in response to new access points, using examples from 2018 to demonstrate both success and failure.

Edexcel	UK Politics 1.3	How different pressure groups exert influence and how their methods and influence vary in contemporary politics
		Case studies of two different pressure groups, highlighting examples of how their methods and influence vary
AQA	3.1.2.4	A detailed study of one insider and one outsider group
		Methods used by pressure groups

Context

Traditional wisdom on pressure groups has relied heavily on the work of Stewart in 1958 and Grant's seminal work of 1989. Stewart classified pressure groups as 'sectional' groups, representing the common interests of a section of society, and 'causal' groups, promoting an idea. Grant divided pressure groups into 'insiders' and 'outsiders'. These classifications were to some extent either a result of pressure group action, or determined how they might act in order to preserve their status. Grant's considerable later work, however, identified not only the developing and evolutionary nature of pressure groups and actions, but used this to identify flaws in the original typology. The rise in direct action and growth in technology and the internet has created tensions over the methods of traditional 'insider groups'. These changes have given rise to a category of 'new social movements' by some theorists. These are broad movements, such as the fight for LGBTQ rights, which are more loosely organised and fight for social change.

The twenty-first century saw these challenges to the classifications continue due to the changes in method. The introduction of a Supreme Court in the UK, effective from October 2009, has given groups a high-profile judicial route to try to achieve their aims. The increase in devolution has increased the number of access points available to groups for lobbying. The internet has allowed not only for cheap and swift mass action, such as e-petitions, but also allowed for greater coordination of direct action as well as the growth of crowdfunding for issues. All of this has served to allow 'traditional' membership groups to be challenged by more loosely organised movements or single-issue campaigns. It has also allowed for individuals to create considerable pressure alone, which can be utilised, or added to, by more traditional groups.

Pressure groups and e-democracy

Pressure groups have been able to take advantage of advances in technology to further their causes, and the role of the internet is increasingly crucial, whether by responding to government consultations regarding legislation, signing an e-petition, donating to crowdfunding, or using it to organise a more traditional form of protest.

Crowdfunding allows individuals to donate small amounts of money via the internet to advance a cause with which they have sympathy. This has typically been used to fund expensive processes such as launching a judicial review. Crowdfunding has historic roots that go back centuries, but the advances of technology and websites such as Crowd Justice and Go Fund Me have meant this is not only more widely used, but also more well-known by the public at large. Obviously, having money alone is no guarantee of success for a pressure group. However, this is a developing revenue stream for many groups. Having such money allows them to undertake more costly activities, such as legal challenges. The total cost of the Asher's Bakery case, for example, was around £500,000, showing that funding support is necessary if groups are to be able to mount a challenge.

Table 5.1 Crowdfunding, the judiciary and campaigns in 2018

Campaign	Success?
Challenge to civil partnerships only being available for same-sex couples, October 2018	SUCCESS — Charles Keidan and Rebecca Steinfeld raised nearly £40,000 on Go Fund Me, and won their challenge in the UK Supreme Court in the summer of 2018, which the government then agreed to write into UK law in October.
Challenge to the legality of Britain's decision to leave the EU — June 2018	FAILURE — Elizabeth Webster raised nearly £200,000 on Crowd Justice to launch an appeal in the High Court. This was rejected by the High Court.
Challenge to government's Investigatory Powers Act ('Snooper's Charter'), April 2018	SUCCESS — Pressure group Liberty used Crowd Justice to raise over £50,000 to launch this challenge. The High Court ruled the Act was incompatible with EU law, meaning the government has 6 months to rewrite it.

Campaign	Success?
Challenge to the government's 'right to rent' scheme, December 2018	TO BE DECIDED — the Joint Council for the Welfare of Immigrants raised around £4,000 on Crowd Justice to challenge the 'hostile environment' this policy created towards immigrants. Trial set in the High Court for December 2018.
Challenge to government badger cull, August 2018	FAILURE — Tom Langton raised nearly £15,000 on Crowd Justice for a High Court challenge to limit the government's badger cull. The High Court ruled against this challenge, allowing for the extension of the badger cull.

Most notably given the current political circumstances, groups such as the People's Vote have used the internet to gather support for a referendum on the final Brexit deal. By the end of September 2018, it had gained over 300,000 signatures on its website whilst an independent-backed petition for the same issue on Change.org had gained nearly 900,000 signatures. Mass pressure as a way to galvanise government action is nothing new, but the ubiquity of the internet has allowed it to become far more common.

Box 5.1 The demands of the People's Vote

We have watched the chaos unfold in Cabinet and the turmoil in negotiations with dismay and foreboding. None of us voted for a bad deal or no deal that would wreck our economy. Nor do we accept that either is inevitable. If the Brexit deal is rejected by Parliament, then we, the people of Britain, should have the democratic right to determine our own future. That is why we are demanding a People's Vote on the final Brexit deal.

The highs and lows of the internet

The internet allows pressure to become a key part of pluralist democracy. It also enables vast numbers of people to take part in democratic action, encouraging engagement and education without having to expend a lot of time, energy or money. This widening of participation should allow for a more accountable government and dispersal of power. There are considerable questions to be raised, however, over the extent to which such action is political participation. The signing of petitions or micro-donations of crowdfunding are so relatively quick and simple that they could be labelled 'clicktivism', meaning taking part through the click of a mouse. The number e-petitions signed or even created in the UK annually contrasts sharply with the low party membership figures and turnout rates at elections. People are not really engaging politically online with pressure groups; rather they are delegating their power and authority to them through a signature or donation. Even the Brexit referendum only managed a turnout of 72%, which was considered high.

The growth of petitions can also water down their effectiveness. A search on the Parliament's own petitions website returns no less than 684 petitions that include 'Brexit', varying in signatories from nearly 150,000 to just 21. In addition, the petitions are contradictory and nuanced — for and against Brexit, or covering smaller policy areas such as 'include cycle paths in post-Brexit farming subsidies'. Equally, on Crowd Justice in 2018, there were 13 separate cases of crowdfunding for a legal issue to do with Brexit raising nearly £900,000. This dispersal of power between disparate groups makes their chances of success notably lower.

Even the more traditional methods of pressure group action, such as protests and strikes, must be aware of the impact of the internet. With the continuing advances in 24-hour news and the need for exciting headlines, how these events are reported can have a direct impact on success. Robert Peston, ITV's political editor, commented that a protest of over 1,000 head teachers was too well behaved. His tweet, whilst missing out the word 'impossible', seemed to suggest that their good behaviour actually made it impossible to make an interesting headline news story from their protest. The head teachers were protesting over funding cuts to schools, which amount to 8% in real terms since 2010. The BBC who did manage a story on this protest headlined it, 'Head teachers' polite protest over funding in England'. Such reactions obviously have an impact on pressure groups methods. The main aim of such protests is to highlight a cause to the public and both demonstrate and create a groundswell of sympathy — this is rather challenging when to make such headlines, a level of civil disobedience seems to be required, which serves to undermine the legitimacy of the movement. The internet has not only opened new methods for pressure groups, but it is forcing them to evolve traditional methods too.

Box 5.2 Robert Peston's tweet regarding the head teachers' strike

Memo to head teachers: next time you go on a protest march, it might be sensible to do some protesting. My colleagues tell me you were so well-behaved — presumably so as not to set a bad example to your students (!) — that you've made it almost [impossible] for us to make a TV news piece.

Pressure groups and the Supreme Court

As with crowdfunding, the Supreme Court is not necessarily a 2018 'development', but is certainly becoming a more prominent access point for pressure groups to utilise. There were more high profile cases coming from the Supreme Court, and more regular headlines in the media on the impact of their rulings than ever before. Many cases in the court are brought and fought by individuals rather than pressure groups. However, many pressure groups have a role in either promoting the case to their followers being asked for comments for news articles, or providing funding to allow individuals to proceed with their cases. In the latter, groups provide funding often because the outcome of such a case is directly relevant to them. Supporting cases brought by individuals are a vehicle for them to achieve outcomes in line with the goals of their group.

Table 5.2 Supreme Court rulings in 2018

Case	Outcome	Group/s involved
Pimlico Plumbers *Pimlico Plumbers Ltd* v *Smith*	'Self-employed' workers in the gig-economy are entitled to workers' benefits.	Funded by the Equality and Human Rights Commission.
Civil partnerships for mixed-sex couples *Steinfeld and Keidan v Secretary of State for International Development*	Same-sex only civil partnerships were unlawful.	Equal Civil Partnerships fight the same cause, and has a direct link to Steinfeld/Keidan's petition on its website.
Abortion in Northern Ireland Judicial Review — Northern Ireland Human Rights Commission	Supreme Court ruled against the Commission which was challenging the legality of Northern Ireland's abortion law.	The case was brought by the Northern Ireland Human Rights Commission.
Asher's Bakery *Lee* v *Asher's Baking Company Ltd*	The case of a bakery that refused to make a cake with the slogan 'Support gay marriage' on religious grounds has been heard. The Court found in favour of Asher's Bakery.	Funded by the Christian Institute's Legal Defence Fund.
Alfie Evans In the matter of Alfie Evans No. 2	Supreme Court denied an appeal that Alfie Evans was being unlawfully detained in hospital.	Alfie Evans' parents were represented by lawyers from the Christian Legal Centre.

The status of and knowledge about the Supreme Court has certainly improved since the Gina Miller case. However, its power is still firmly rooted in statute, rather than a written constitution like its US counterpart. This means that whilst it is becoming more widely utilised, the rulings it makes do not have sovereignty and they have no power to force Parliament to act. Equally, the precedent set by Supreme Court rulings does not have the breadth that rulings in the US have. In the case of Pimlico Plumbers, whilst it is likely to have an impact on businesses such as Uber and Deliveroo, the ruling is not immediately applicable to them. The reality, however, is that given the increased status of the Supreme Court, Parliament is unlikely to ignore it, although it certainly is not impossible.

In order to successfully launch an action such as this in the Supreme Court, a great deal of legal support is needed. This comes at a cost. On the one hand, the Supreme Court is able to bring a great deal of pressure on the UK government with its rulings. This enhances liberal democracy by serving as a limit on the government and ensuring that rights are protected. However, in order to be able to do so, individuals must either be individually wealthy or well funded. This rather makes the Supreme Court an elitist access point, available only to those groups and individuals that are able to afford it. This runs counter to the pluralist democracy that is to some extent created by the internet, and yet it affords individuals a more high profile way to challenge the government.

Comparison: pressure group action in the UK and the USA

Pressure groups in the USA have long had access to a vast array of access points due to the separated branches of government, frequent election cycle and federal nature of the USA. Comparatively, UK groups have found their access points growing in number in recent years. However, the methods and influence of these groups remain similar, perhaps not surprisingly given both countries operate under the principles of representative and liberal democracy.

- The increasing profile of the UK Supreme Court makes this access point similar to that of the US Supreme Court, both hearing cases brought by pressure groups to achieve their aims more broadly.
- The much shorter US election cycle means that the role of pressure groups and the money they can donate to achieve their policy aims are far more influential in the USA than in the UK.

Edexcel	Comparative Politics 6.2.9	The relative power, methods and influence of pressure groups.
AQA	3.2.2.5	The relative power, influence and methods of pressure groups in the UK and the USA

Summary

Pressure group activity in the UK continues to play a major role not just in government policy-making but also in the UK media. A key debate, however, is they type of democracy supported by pressure groups. The growth of e-democracy seems to support pluralism, and yet the dilution of concentration through this methods potentially hampers its success. Comparatively the Supreme Court supports both an elitist and liberal democracy but is unavailable to a great many citizens of the UK. There is a great tensions between these newly developing access points and the effect they have on democracy in UK.

Further debates include:

- whether the role of technology is an evolution in pressure groups tactics or simply a quicker way of achieving traditional ends
- whether it is necessary to reevaluate traditional pressure group classifications given developments in the twenty-first century

- the necessity of pressure groups in a pluralist democracy
- the effectiveness of pressure groups within the democratic process
- the role and significance of the breadth of access points available for pressure group use

Further reading and research

- Read the Democratic Audit's account of pressure groups and democracy, 'How democratic is the interest group process in the UK?, 24 August 2018, **democraticaudit.com**.
- Research the timeline of civil partnerships, from their creation in 2004 to the government decision in October 2018.
- Find out more about the recent impact — success or failure — of crowdfunding over a range of areas at **www.crowdjustice.com**.
- Aiming for an A? Compare the actions of head teachers and Heathrow protesters by looking at the articles below on **www.bbc.co.uk**. What are the benefits of each method?
  - 'Heathrow airport: MPs vote in favour of expansion', 26 June 2018
  - 'Head teachers' polite protest over funding in England', Hannah Richardson, 28 September 2018

Chapter 6

Parliament: how effective was parliamentary scrutiny of the executive in 2018?

Exam success

The examination specifications focus on the relationship between Parliament and the executive, requiring analysis of how effectively the executive is held to account. The best candidates will focus not just on the prime minister, but also look at the cabinet, evaluating a range of methods that Parliament can employ to scrutinise the executive as a whole, as well as remembering that Parliament consists both of the House of Commons and House of Lords. Top answers will analytically deploy unique examples from 2018 to demonstrate the evolution and flexibility that Parliament demonstrates in exercising scrutiny.

Edexcel	UK Government 2.4	The ways in which Parliament interacts with the executive
	UK Government 4.2	The influence and effectiveness of Parliament in holding the executive to account
		The extent to which the balance of power between Parliament and the executive has changed.
AQA	3.1.1.2	Scrutiny of the executive and how effective scrutiny of the executive is in practice

Context

From Montesquieu's 1748 pivotal text, *De l'esprit des lois*, comes the argument for a government of three separate branches. This should ensure that no one branch can gain too much power and influence over either of the others or over the political liberty of their citizens. The UK government does not fit this model. The executive and legislation branches are 'fused' with the prime minister and cabinet drawn mostly from the elected representatives of the majority party in the House of Commons. Historically, it has been argued that this has allowed for the possibility of an 'elective dictatorship', with parliamentary scrutiny being largely ineffective.

For most of the last decade however, the number of backbench rebellions has notably increased, the House of Lords has become more aggressive and the role and power of select committees has garnered much greater press attention. Significant reforms of Parliament have also taken place, in part to develop its influence over the executive. Notably, the Wright Reforms made select committees electable by secret ballot, going some way to relieving them of the influence of the party whip, and created a Backbench Business Committee to give backbenchers greater control over the agenda and debates of the House of Commons.

In 2018, this continued to develop, with archaic parliamentary laws being used to scrutinise the government in new and novel ways. Despite this, concerns remain over how truly effective Parliament is at scrutiny, and whether this role will continue to develop, or is simply a result of electoral results of the last decade.

Did scrutiny of the executive develop and change in 2018?

The issue of Brexit continued to dominate parliamentary proceedings in 2018, and it was this issue that gave rise to a number of new and surprisingly innovative ways in which the opposition tried to scrutinise the executive.

The humble address

The humble address is formally know as 'a motion for return'. This archaic principle can be found in *Parliamentary Practice* by Thomas Erskine May, one of the fundamental authoritative works of the UK constitution. It has been rarely used in recent decades but made an astonishing return in 2018 opposition days. Under Standing Order 14, 20 days are allocated to the opposition each year – on 17 of those days, the leader of the opposition determines the agenda, and the remaining 3 days are given to the second largest party. On these days, members of the opposition can schedule a humble address, a request made to the monarch for a release of government documents. As her majesty's government, this address effectively requests documents of the current government. Crucially, votes on humble addresses are accepted as binding on the government.

Table 6.1 Humble addresses in parliament, 1997–2018

Parliament	Number of humble addresses
1997–2010: Labour government	0
2010–15: Coalition government	0
2015–17: Conservative government	0
2017–: Conservative minority government	6 • exiting the EU • Universal Credit • Carillion • EU exit analysis • Windrush • NHS outsourcing and privatisation

The humble address has only been rarely used in any Parliament in the last 200 years. However, at the end of 2017 it made headlines when the Shadow Brexit secretary Sir Keir Starmer (Labour) used it to petition for the release of 58 government studies reviewing the possible economic impact of Brexit on the UK.

> **Box 6.1** **Case study: Sir Keir Starmer and the Brexit humble address**
>
> On 1 November 2017, the Shadow Brexit Secretary Sir Keir Starmer tabled a humble address to petition her majesty, and by extension her majesty's government, to release 58 studies conducted into the potential economic impact of Brexit on the UK. He wanted these given over to the Brexit select committee to allow it to carry out appropriate scrutiny of the government Brexit policy, whilst ministers argued that they should not be released as they could create difficulties in the continuing negotiations with the EU. In keeping with May's policy not to contest opposition day motions, this humble address passed Parliament without a division. The humble address was effectively supported by the Speaker of the House of Commons John Bercow, who advised the government that such addresses were binding on them.
>
> Starmer's timetabled motion was 'That an humble Address be presented to Her Majesty, That she will be graciously pleased to give directions that the list of sectors analysed under the instruction of Her Majesty's Ministers, and referred to in the Answer of 26 June 2017 to Question 239, be laid before this House and that the impact assessments arising from those analyses be provided to the Committee on Exiting the European Union'.

Following Starmer's address, the humble address has been used a further five times in this Parliament, a notable increase. Of the six humble addresses that have been put on the opposition agenda since November 2017, the government did not contest four of them, allowing them to pass without division, whilst two (NHS privatisation and Windrush) were voted upon and both were won by the government.

This suggests that in the face of government intransigence over Brexit, Parliament has looked for new ways in which it can shore up its power and mount suitable challenges against the government. The success of this, however, is debatable. Humble addresses are only binding if they pass, and therefore a government with a majority should be able to defeat them. In the case of Brexit, whilst the papers have been released to parliamentarians, only 6% of them have requested access to the papers, questioning the depth of scrutiny going on beyond the headlines.

Opposition days

Opposition days are 20 days in the annual parliamentary calendar on which the second and third biggest parties in the House of Commons decide on the agenda for the day. They are not a new addition to the powers of parliamentary scrutiny, but the government's reaction to them in 2017 and 2018 was a change from the norm. Motions put forward on opposition days often have little chance of success as whilst the opposition controls the agenda, the government maintains its majority so the chances of anything passing are slim. Most commonly they are used instead to raise the profile of an issue.

The current government has taken the unusual step of choosing not to contest votes on opposition day motions. This is due to the fact that the Conservative Party does not have a majority and therefore could face embarrassing defeats in these motions. Unlike humble addresses, opposition day motions are not binding. If the government were defeated in these votes therefore, it would not have to honour any vote, but it would make it look exceptionally weak. The Speaker John Bercow nonetheless criticised the government for taking this action.

Table 6.2 Opposition day motions in parliament, 1997–2018

Parliament	Number of opposition day motions	Number of government defeats in division	Government defeats in division (%)	Number of government defeats without division	Government defeats without division (%)
1997–2010 Labour	413	1	0	7	2
2010–15 Coalition	168	2	1	21	13
2015–17 Conservative	73	2	3	6	8
2017–* Conservative minority	20	4	20	14	70

* Data to 24 May 2018

This has served to undermine the power that Parliament has to scrutinise government in this way. Traditionally opposition days have been a way to raise issues governments have chosen to avoid, such as the 2014 motion regarding the crisis in the Passport Office which attracted such media attention that the government was forced to re-take control of this office. However, with the government effectively opting out of participating in these debates, the extent to which Parliament can effectively scrutinise the government becomes limited. On the rare occasions that the current government has taken part in votes on opposition day motions, they have been victorious:

- Motion that government should release the Brexit customs plans – government defeated the motion 301–269.
- Motion regarding the government handing of the East Coast Rail franchise – government defeated the motion 304–271.

The ability of the government to secure victories in these votes at a time when it has no outright majority serves to outline the limitations of opposition days as an effective method of scrutiny.

Box 6.2 John Bercow responds to the government opting out of opposition day votes, October 2017

If you choose not to take part and vote you can't say, 'well, we didn't lose'. A minister from the government should come to the House and show respect to the institution and say what it intends to do. This institution is bigger than any one party and is bigger than any government.

The rise and rise of select committees

Under the Wright Committee reforms, select committees in Parliament were strengthened. In 2018, they were able to use their investigatory powers to highlight a number of government shortcomings with notable success, for example:

- **Home Affairs Select Committee and Amber Rudd, April 2018:** the Windrush scandal surrounded the potential deportation of people who had come to Britain from Commonwealth countries as children but lacked British citizenship paperwork. As the scandal mounted, Amber Rudd faced questions from this committee regarding the setting of targets of deportation. Whilst she denied such targets existed, a leaked memo suggested that a memo had been prepared for Rudd outlining the targets; just 2 days later she resigned.

- **David Davis and the Exiting the European Union Select Committee, October 2017**: in giving evidence to this select committee, David Davis, as the secretary of state for exiting the European Union, was asked by Semma Malhotra (Labour) to outline the timeline for Brexit. His answer suggested that Parliament might not get a vote until after the UK had exited the European Union. By midday, this matter was a question at PMQs. By mid-afternoon, Davis' department had had to issue a statement reassuring Parliament it should expect to have a vote before the UK left the EU. By the following morning, Davis was summoned to Parliament to answer an urgent question.

There has also been a growing number of select committees working together on investigations to give more weight to their recommendations. In an unprecedented move in March 2018, four select committees came together to issue a report demanding an end to the UK's 'poisonous air', the first time four committees had come together and collaborated on such a report. The four committees involved – Environment, Health, Transport and the Environmental Audit Committee – complained that air pollution caused early deaths and annually cost the UK £20bn. Their report was also notable coming after the government had lost a number of court cases, including one as recently as February 2018, requiring the government to take more action to tackle air pollution.

The weakness remains that the government is under no obligation to accept the recommendations of select committees. However, the increasing profile that the reports of these committees have in the press, in addition to high profile witnesses, make their recommendations more difficult to ignore. Even witnesses refusing to attend can make headlines – Mark Zuckerberg's refusal to give evidence to the Digital, Culture, Media and Sport Select Committee was described as 'absolutely astonishing' by the committee's chair in the wake of the Analytica scandal. All of this can add considerable pressure for the government to act, even if the committees themselves do not have the pressure to force such action.

| Box 6.3 | **Amber Rudd giving evidence to the Home Affairs Select Committee which ultimately led to her resignation, April 2018** |

Amber Rudd: If you're asking me are there numbers of people that we expect to be removed, that's not how we operate. I do think it is right — I know we are talking about Windrush here, who are legal migrants — but where there are people here that are here illegally, it is right that we do try to remove them.

Yvette Cooper (committee chair): OK, so we've just had very clear evidence, so I think we need to clear this up very quickly because if there are removals targets in the Home Office and the two people who are supposedly in charge don't know about them then that feels pretty serious and feels like a lack of grip anywhere in the system.

Comparison: the role of Parliament and Congress in executive oversight

Parliament and Congress do have similar roles in maintaining oversight of the executive branch. However, in 2018, Congress made President Trump's time in office considerably more challenging than Parliament made Prime Minister May's:

- Whilst May faced humiliating defeats in the Lords over the Brexit Bill, many of these were reversed in the House of Commons despite her lack of a majority. Trump by comparison failed to achieve his 'repeal and replace' of Obamacare, despite holding a Republican majority in both houses of Congress.
- Despite lacking a majority, party divisions and cabinet resignations, May's government continued relatively intact. The investigations by four congressional committees into Russian hacking, and subsequent investigation from the Justice Department headed by Robert Mueller, led to damning indictments of staff close to Trump, and posed considerable problems for Trump's reputation and polling numbers, the lowest of any president at 100 days and 1 year in office.
- Investigations by UK committees have proved to be a thorn in May's side, but their achievements are relatively minor and government has continued. The antagonism between President Trump and Congress reached a head in January 2018 when the USA suffered two (short) government shutdowns.

Edexcel	Comparative Politics 6.2.3	Comparison of the US and UK legislative branches and their resulting impact on politics and government powers; strengths and weaknesses of each of the Houses
AQA	3.2.2.1	The legislatures: their relative strengths and weaknesses and the extent to which their roles are similar and their powers equal

Summary

The challenges of Parliament's ability to hold the government to account clearly remain present. Its ability to devise new ways of trying to make this an effective power suggest it has yet to find a way that is truly and consistently effective. In a system with fused powers and in which the government usually maintains a majority in Parliament, it is likely that this will remain a problem. However, in a decade when the electoral system has consistently returned small, or no, majorities in Parliament, and with the addition of parliamentary reforms, it is evident that this power is one that Parliament values and is working to constantly evolve. Further debates include:

- whether there needs to be further reforms to strengthen the powers of parliamentary scrutiny including whether the Wright Committee reforms went far enough
- whether party political scrutiny can be considered effective, or merely for political gain
- how strong the powers of Parliament actually are if it is relying on media reporting to put pressure upon the government, and the appropriateness of this
- the legitimacy of the House of Lords in scrutinising an elected government
- the success of both liberal and representative democracy in the UK given the current level of parliamentary scrutiny

Further reading and research

- Read the UCL Constitution Unit's, 'Labour's "motion for a return": what and why?', 10 November 2017 on www.constitution-unit.com.
- Go to www.revolts.co.uk to research the trends of backbench rebellions.
- Find out more about different types of parliamentary scrutiny by visiting www.parliament.uk.
- Aiming for an A? Compare the LSE and Democratic Audit's assessment of parliamentary effectiveness:
  - 'How effective is Parliament in controlling UK government and representing citizens?' — click on 'LSE Comment' on http://blogs.lse.ac.uk
  - 'Audit 2017: How effective is the Westminster Parliament in scrutinising central government policy-making?', 31 August 2017, www.democraticaudit.com

Chapter 7

Prime minister and cabinet: 12 months of ministerial resignations — what, who, why and how?

Exam success

The examination specifications focus on both collective ministerial responsibility and individual ministerial responsibility. These two concepts also help to explain the relationship between the cabinet and the prime minister and can be used to debate how significant the cabinet and its members actually are. The best candidates will be able to clearly differentiate between these two concepts, and be able to evaluate examples of each. They will also be able explain why the actions of a minister can have a direct influence on the role and power of the prime minister. Top answers will look at the vast number and range of examples from 2018 to demonstrate the precarious nature of prime ministerial power in a minority government, especially in the controversial era of Brexit.

Edexcel	UK Government 3.2	The concept of ministerial responsibility
	UK Government 3.3.1	Factors that affect the relationship between the prime minister and cabinet
AQA	3.1.1.3	The difference between individual and collective responsibility
		The relationship between prime minister and cabinet

Context

Cabinet collective responsibility has roots in the eighteenth century. The 'Glorious Revolution' had limited but not eliminated the power of the monarch. In the face of one-on-one meetings with the king, government ministers agreed beforehand on their policies to ensure that they could maintain power over the monarch. In the twenty-first century, the necessity of cabinet collective responsibility is outlined in the *Ministerial Code*, with the January 2018 edition stating that: 'Decisions reached by the cabinet or ministerial committees are binding on all members of the government.' Publically therefore cabinet members should support and defend decisions taken by the cabinet, regardless of their personal opinion.

Since 2010, this concept has been troublesome. It was suspended under the Coalition government. After 2015, it was difficult to maintain given the small majority the Conservatives held and divisions within the party over Brexit. These divisions have only deepened. Following a snap election in 2017, the enacting of Article 50 and the sharp controversy over the Chequers plan, a spate of ministers have spoken openly in defiance of the cabinet and a significant number of cabinet resignations have resulted.

Individual ministerial responsibility is also documented in the *Ministerial Code*, stating: 'Ministers have a duty to Parliament to account, and be held to account, for the policies, decisions and actions of their departments and agencies.' This requires that ministers take responsibility for all of the actions of the department that they run. They should explain their department's actions, apologise and even resign if necessary.

Whilst 2018 saw at least one resignation due to individual ministerial responsibility, it also saw resignations due to personal misconduct of ministers. Between 2010 and 2014, Cameron faced just one or two resignations from cabinet ministers annually. Since 1 November 2017, Theresa May has seen seven cabinet ministers resign, and since 13 June 2018 the total includes a further seven non-cabinet minister resignations and the resignation of four private parliamentary secretaries.

The key resignations of 2017–18

The most substantial reason for the high number of resignations under May has been the issue of Brexit. This accounts for the loss of two cabinet secretaries, three non-cabinet ministers and four private parliamentary secretaries. However, policy and personal scandals also cost ministers their roles.

Table 7.1 Cabinet resignations

Parliament	Number of cabinet-level resignations
1997–2001: Labour (Blair)	5
2001–05: Labour (Blair)	7
2005–07: Labour (Blair)	1
2007–10: Labour (Brown)	9
2010–15: Coalition (Cameron)	6
2015–16: Conservative (Cameron)	1
2016–17: Conservative (May)	0
2017– current: Conservative (May)	9 (by November 2018)

Table 7.2 The cabinet of Theresa May, 2017–18

Portfolio	June 2017	Change	November 2018
Prime minister	Theresa May	Position held	Theresa May
Minister for the Cabinet Office	Damian Green	No longer in the cabinet	David Lidington CBE
Chancellor of the exchequer	Philip Hammond	Position held	Philip Hammond

Portfolio	June 2017	Change	November 2018
Home secretary	Amber Rudd	Resigned from cabinet	Sajid Javid
Foreign secretary	Boris Johnson	No longer in the cabinet	Jeremy Hunt
'Brexit' secretary	David Davis	No longer in the cabinet	New to cabinet — Stephen Barclay
Defence secretary	Sir Michael Fallon	No longer in the cabinet	Gavin Williamson CBE
Health secretary	Jeremy Hunt	Moved to foreign secretary	New to cabinet — Matthew Hancock
Justice secretary	David Lidington CBE	Moved to Cabinet Office	David Gauke
Education secretary	Justine Greening	No longer in the cabinet	Damien Hinds
International trade secretary	Liam Fox	Position held	Liam Fox
Business secretary	Greg Clark	Position held	Greg Clark
Environment secretary	Michael Gove	Position held	Michael Gove
Transport secretary	Chris Grayling	Position held	Chris Grayling
Housing and communities secretary	Sajid Javid	Moved to home secretary	James Brokenshire
Leader of the House of Lords	The Baroness Evans of Bowes Park PC	Position held	The Baroness Evans of Bowes Park PC
Scottish secretary	David Mundell	Position held	David Mundell
Welsh secretary	Alun Cairns	Position held	Alun Cairns
Northern Irish secretary	James Brokenshire	Moved to Housing and Communities	Karen Bradley
International development secretary	Priti Patel	No longer in the cabinet	New to cabinet — Penny Mordaunt
Culture secretary	Karen Bradley	Moved to Northern Irish	Jeremy Wright
Works and pensions secretary	David Gauke	Moved to Justice	Returned to cabinet — Amber Rudd
Leader of the House of Commons	Andrea Leadsom	Position held	Andrea Leadsom

Portfolio	June 2017	Change	November 2018
Chief secretary to the treasury	Elizabeth Truss	Position held	Elizabeth Truss
Chief whip	Gavin Williamson	Moved to Defence	New to cabinet — Julian Smith
Attorney general	Jeremy Wright	Moved to Culture	New to cabinet — Geoffrey Cox
Minister of state for immigration	Brandon Lewis*		New to cabinet — Caroline Noakes
Minister of state for employment	Damien Hinds	Moved to Education	New to cabinet — Claire Perry

* Minister without portfolio and chairman of the Conservative Party in September 2018

Amber Rudd: the misleading Parliament resignation

The Windrush generation are British citizens who arrived in the UK after the Second World War from Commonwealth countries. Their name derives from the ship which brought them to the UK and they had their rights guaranteed in the 1971 Immigration Act. Many of these people, however, lacked documentation to prove their status. A raft of changes at the Home Office to their policy led to members of the Windrush generation, legal citizens of Britain many of whom were UK taxpayers, being faced with deportation or facing huge medical bills as they were unable to prove they were citizens.

Under the principle of individual ministerial responsibility, minister's must not only accept responsibility for the actions of their department, they are also expected to give a truthful account of any issues to Parliament if asked. Rudd was called to give evidence in front of the Home Affairs Select Committee over the scandal. At this hearing she gave evidence that there were no targets for the number of illegal immigrants removed from the UK. It quickly became apparent from a leaked memo, which had been prepared for Rudd, that a target had been set for 2017–18. For misleading Parliament, Rudd resigned from the cabinet at the end of April 2018.

The scandal left May with little option but to accept Rudd's resignation. However, in doing so, Rudd also took the blame for some of the more illiberal policies put forward by May herself. Some described her resignation as a loss of May's 'human shield'.

Box 7.1 Excerpt from Amber Rudd's resignation letter

It is with great regret that I am resigning as home secretary. I feel it is necessary to do so because I inadvertently misled the Home Affairs Select Committee over targets for removal of illegal immigrants during their questions on Windrush.

Since appearing before the select committee, I have reviewed the advice I was given on this issue and become aware of information provided to my office which makes mention of targets. I should have been aware of this, and I take full responsibility for the fact that I was not.

Justine Greening: the 'I won't be moved' resignation

Justine Greening had been the education secretary. In a cabinet reshuffle in 2018, she was offered a new post at the Department of Work and Pensions. There were rumours that Greening was to be moved for not being supportive enough of May's education policies and for being too outspoken at cabinet meetings. However, whilst May wanted to move her, Greening was not so acquiescent. She spent nearly 3 hours in Downing Street defending her desire to remain as the secretary for education. Whilst health secretary Jeremy Hunt proved it was possible to argue for staying in his role, Greening was not successful. She ultimately refused to take up the new post offered to her and resigned from the cabinet.

The case of Greening underlined the dangers of cabinet for a prime minister. May ultimately could not create the new cabinet that she wanted following a reshuffle. The loss of Greening from the cabinet also freed her from cabinet collective responsibility. As a remainer, this has allowed Greening the freedom to take swipes at May's policies, embodied in her comments that it has been more than 30 years since the Conservatives had 'connected with people's aspirations'.

Michael Fallon: the personal life resignation

Michael Fallon was May's defence secretary. In October 2017, a number of allegations surfaced in parliament of serious sexual abuse including allegations against Michael Fallon. These initially became a source of controversy in the press due to the nature of the allegations against him. An allegation that he had touched the knee of a journalist at a conference 15 years ago split public opinion, especially in the wake of the #MeToo campaign. Some saw it as assault, whilst some saw it as an overreaction to a minor event.

However, when journalist Jane Merrick called Downing Street with allegations that he 'had lunged at her and attempted to kiss her on the lips', Fallon's resignation followed shortly thereafter at the beginning of November. Whilst Fallon denied some of the allegations, he said: 'I accept that in the past I have fallen below the high standards that we require of the Armed Forces that I have the honour to represent.'

The scandal led to claims that May's minority government was close to collapse, and this was furthered by the Priti Patel scandal that would follow shortly after. However, it also gave May an opportunity to demonstrate the reaction she had been calling for to the wider sexual abuse allegations — a 'serious, swift, cross-party response this issue demands'.

Priti Patel: the acting alone resignation

Priti Patel had been May's international development secretary. However, in November 2017, after nearly a week of headlines, Patel was forced to resign over meetings she had held with Israeli ministers. The meetings in themselves may have fallen within her remit. However, she met with these ministers, including the Israeli prime minister Benjamin Netanyahu, unofficially whilst she was supposedly on a family holiday. That these meetings had not been authorised in advance and no other UK officials were present was the cause of the controversy.

Patel was called to answer an urgent question in the House of Commons over her actions (although a minister from the department was sent instead) and on the same day it becomes clear that Patel had not been completely open about her Israeli meetings with May. This scandal occurred in the same week as Fallon's sex scandal, and whilst Damian Green was being investigated over similar allegations. Patel was summoned to Downing Street for just a 6-minute meeting and resigned the same evening.

In the wake of policy scandals such as this, the lack of power May had over the actions of her cabinet not only became apparent, but showed the headache that ministerial resignations such as this can cause for power of the prime minister.

Box 7.2 Theresa May's response to Patel's resignation

But that [working closely with Israel] must be done formally, and through official channels. That is why, when we met on Monday, I was glad to accept your apology and welcomed your clarification about your trip to Israel over the summer.

Now that further details have come to light, it is right that you have decided to resign and adhere to the high standards of transparency and openness that you have advocated.

Boris Johnson and David Davis: the policy resignation

Within 24 hours of one another, the secretary for exiting the European Union and the foreign secretary resigned over May's Brexit plan, known as the 'Chequers plan'. May had clearly expected the plan, laid out on the 6 July 2018 at Chequers, to meet some resistance. She purportedly warned cabinet members that if they resigned at the meeting they would lose their ministerial car and face a long taxi ride home including a 1-mile walk down the Chequers driveway. Nonetheless, just days later both Johnson and Davis had resigned.

Davis said that he did not believe in the plan laid out at Chequers, feeling that the UK was 'giving away too much and too easily' and it seeming more unlikely that the UK would leave the customs union. May was very clear that she did not agree, but the resignation as a huge blow as she tried to deal with the divisions between the Brexiteers and the remainers within her party.

The very next day, Johnson also resigned, claiming the plan would leave the UK with 'the status of a colony'. Not only was his resignation a challenge given his high status and outspoken nature, but he also broke with convention, releasing his resignation letter before Downing Street had a chance to reply. May also had to face the House of Commons after his resignation, where she reiterated that she expected cabinet members to conform to collective responsibility.

The resignations led to numerous rumours about possible leadership challenges to May, which would have needed 48 MPs to write letters of no confidence to the 1922 Committee. However, this did not come to fruition. Nonetheless, it threw May's Brexit negotiations into chaos.

How did May survive?

Given the stark number of cabinet resignations, that May survived is itself surprising. These resignations demonstrate a variety of weaknesses in her power over the cabinet and in their usefulness for her. However, in a time of public division over Brexit, a lack of coordination from the Labour Party over their own proposed Brexit plan and a lack of a plan from the Brexiteers themselves, May might simply be the best of a bad situation at the moment.

Comparison: the UK and US cabinets

The UK and US cabinets are starkly contrasted. Whilst the UK cabinet is governed by collective responsibility and has considerable power, the US cabinet is not at all collective and has no constitutional power.

The resignations of Johnson and Davis over their personal dislike of May's Brexit policy were similar to the resignation of Chuck Hagel as defense secretary under Obama. He disagreed with Obama's policies on Guantanamo Bay and the release of detainees. In both cases, the headlines drew public and political attention to these policies.

The pressure from May placed upon her cabinet members before their visit to Chequers could be done by the US President but would seem both unnecessary and unlikely. Obama met with his cabinet just six times in his first year, underlining its lack of power, compared with the collective power of the UK cabinet.

Cabinet resignations in the UK lead to a reshuffle of personnel, and there is no experience required in the policy area. In the US, because cabinet meetings are infrequent and the president alone has the power to direct policy, cabinet resignations lead to a search for suitably qualified and experienced candidates as replacements.

Edexcel	Comparative Politics 6.2.5	Key similarities and differences between the role and powers of the US president and the UK prime minister
AQA	3.2.2.2	The role and powers of the UK prime minister and of the US president

Summary

Whilst May survived these resignations, they certainly left her weaker — with a divided cabinet, outspoken remainers and Brexiteers not bound by collective responsibility and a lack of a parliamentary majority, at the end of 2018 May's position was far from secure. The role of the cabinet for the prime minister does therefore vary dependent on a range of factors.

Further debates include:

- whether collective responsibility can be maintained in an era of small government majorities
- whether individual ministerial responsibility is possible given the size of government and advent of 24-hour media
- the extent to which the leadership skills of a prime minister can overcome cabinet divisions
- the role of political circumstances in cabinet power, including electoral results, national events and political or economic concerns
- whether cabinet remains a significant body given the media focus on the prime minister alone

Further reading and research

- Read the *New Statesman*'s, 'Brexiteer cabinet resignations would be pointless', 6 July 2018, www.new statesman.com.
- Research and compare the resignation of Justine Greening to the continued role of Jeremy Hunt as health secretary in January 2018. What does this suggest about the power of individuals in the cabinet?
- Find and read the *Ministerial Code* online.
- Aiming for an A? Compare the articles below which look at the resignations of Brown, Cameron and May. Explain the resignation trends and how they affected each prime minister:
  - 'Maria Miller makes it six cabinet minister resignations under Cameron', George Arnett, Ami Sedghi and Patrick Scott, 9 April 2014, www.theguardian.com
  - 'Every Tory MP that has resigned so far over Theresa May's Chequers Brexit plan', Karl McDonald, 16 July 2018, www.inews.co.uk

Chapter 8

The judiciary: how did the composition and influence of the Supreme Court change in 2018?

Context

Central to the rule of law — a fundamental principle of the UK's uncodified constitution — is that the law is applied equally, treating all individuals alike regardless of their gender, ethnicity, sexuality, wealth, religion or social status. Consequently, the profile of judges applying the law is of significant interest as the law's application must be free from personal bias. The fact that senior judges tend to share similar, narrow, privileged social and educational backgrounds is regularly highlighted as a threat to judicial neutrality.

An important dimension in the ongoing debate over judicial neutrality is the appointment of senior judges, especially those to the Supreme Court. The Constitutional Reform Act (2005) created the Judicial Appointments Commission (JAC) in 2006, which has the job of selecting candidates for senior judicial office. However, vacancies in the Supreme Court are not filled by the JAC but by a five-member selection commission comprising the president of the Supreme Court, the deputy president of the Supreme Court, one member of the JAC, one member of the Judicial Appointments Board for Scotland, and one member of the Northern Ireland Judicial Appointments Commission.

2018 saw three new appointees fill Supreme Court vacancies. Not only do concerns remain over the composition and diversity of the senior judiciary, but a greater number of sensitive and significant Supreme Court decisions are being made each year — many of them with far-reaching cultural, moral and legal implications.

How did the composition of the Supreme Court change in 2018 and does it matter?

2018 saw the appointment of three new justices to the Supreme Court bench following the retirements of Lord Mance, deputy president of the Court in June 2018, Lord Hughes in August 2018, and Lord Sumption in December 2018. All three departing justices had reached the compulsory retirement age of 75. Judges appointed before 1995 are still permitted to stay on the bench until the age of 75, but those appointed more recently are required to retire at 70.

Prior to these appointments, in December 2017 the information pack for those considering the vacant positions stated that 'applications are sought from the widest range of candidates eligible to apply and particularly those who will increase the diversity of the court'. Nevertheless, on a video message posted on the Supreme Court's website, President of the Court Lady Hale explained that applicants needed to have satisfied the eligibility criteria of holding 'high judicial office' for at least 2 years or to have been a practising solicitor or barrister for at least 15 years, see Box 8.1.

Box 8.1	An excerpt from the president of the Supreme Court, Lady Hale's stated expectations for applicants to join the supreme court

The cases dealt with by the Supreme Court involve difficult points of law of general public importance and demand a deep level of legal knowledge and understanding, combined with high intellectual capacity and an appreciation of the social context in which these issues arise and the communities which the law is there to serve.

Candidates will need also to demonstrate an understanding of the constitutional role of the Supreme Court and its relationship with the other branches of government as well as with the governments and legislatures of Scotland, Wales and Northern Ireland.

The three new justices' appointments were announced on 27 June 2018. Following this, Lady Justice Arden and Lord Justice Kitchin joined the court in October 2018 and Lord Justice Sales followed them in January 2019.

Table 8.1 Supreme Court justices appointed in June 2018

Justice	Date of birth	Age on appointment	University
Dame Mary Arden	21 January 1947	71	Girton College, Cambridge
Sir David Kitchen	30 April 1955	63	Fitzwilliam College, Cambridge
Sir Philip Sales	11 February 1962	56	Churchill College, Cambridge

Table 8.1 provides a snapshot of the age and university background of the recently appointed justices. The *Guardian* commented in June 2018 that the appointment of a third woman to the supreme court bench 'narrowed the gender gap in the UK's highest judicial institution' as Lady Justice Arden — who replaced her husband Lord Mance — joined Lady Hale, the court's president, and the other female justice Lady Black. None of the 12 Supreme Court judges are from black, Asian and minority ethnic (BAME) backgrounds.

Whilst it would be extraordinarily difficult to create a 12-member Supreme Court that is socially representative of the population of the UK, recent appointments have failed to satisfy some who maintain that the senior judicial ranks remain elitist, with little progress being made since Lord Neuberger (then president of the Supreme Court) retired at the end of 2016 stating that: '... the higher echelons of the judiciary in the UK suffer from a marked lack of diversity and... the Supreme Court does not score at all well.'

Even with Lady Arden's appointment, the Supreme Court's gender balance only improved from 16.6% to 25% female. Not only is this worse that the USA, where a third of the US Supreme Court justices are female, but Council of Europe research in its recent report 'Balanced participation of women and men in decision-making' indicates that the UK still has amongst the worst gender balances in European High/Supreme Courts.

However, in late 2018 it was widely reported that for the first time in the 600-year history of the UK's highest court, a female majority would hear a case. Three of the five judges, who heard a Supreme Court case on 3 October 2018 about a 16-year-old with Asperger's syndrome and learning difficulties, were female.

Diversity quotas?
It is widely accepted that appointments to the Supreme Court, as well as to other senior judicial institutions such as the Court of Appeal and High Court, should be based entirely upon merit, but the justice secretary is regularly lobbied by groups seeking a more diverse judicial 'population'.

Diversity quotas remain a controversial subject, with most agreeing that their imposition would be unsuitable for the pinnacles of the profession. However, targets to improve the numbers of female and black, Asian and minority ethnic (BAME) judges at lower judicial levels do have some support. In the Court of Appeal, the highest court within the senior courts of England and Wales and from which the three newly appointed Supreme Court justices were appointed, just a quarter of the 39 Lord and Lady justices are female and there is just one, newly appointed, BAME justice in the Court of Appeal, Lord Justice Singh, appointed in October 2017.

The latest official diversity data, published in the *Judicial Diversity Statistics* (July 2018), indicates that the ranks of the profession are becoming steadily more diverse, but the pace of change is too slow for many campaigners. The President of the Supreme Court, Lady Hale, added to the debate in February 2018 when she called for 'affirmative action rather than positive discrimination' to achieve greater gender and ethnic diversity. For people to have full confidence in the impartiality of the application and administration of justice, judges, said Lady Hale, 'should be as reflective of the population as it is possible to be'.

Supreme Court case studies in 2018: impact and influence

One of the most fundamental powers of the Supreme Court is its ability to use **judicial review** to:

- **clarify the meaning of the law**, especially where disputes or inconsistences occur
- **set legal precedents**, often by reviewing earlier legal precedent and re-establishing common law
- **review the actions of public officials or public bodies** to determine whether they have acted lawfully, often by issuing 'declarations of incompatibility' under the Human Rights Act (1998)
- **determine whether ministers or state bodies have acted *ultra vires***, i.e. beyond the statutory authority granted to them

---

Box 8.2 Case study 1: clarifying the meaning of the law

Pimlico Plumbers Ltd v *Smith* (2018)

In June 2018, the Supreme Court upheld a Court of Appeal decision that a plumber classed as self-employed was in fact a worker. Gary Smith, who paid self-employed tax and was VAT registered, had 'worker status', meaning that he was entitled to various workers' rights such as sick pay, holiday pay and protection from discrimination.

The case hinged on the fact that Pimlico Plumbers required Mr Smith to wear a company branded uniform, to lease one of its vans displaying the company's logo and to work a minimum number of hours per week over a 6-year period.

In a ruling that will continue to have far-reaching consequences, the Supreme Court used its power of judicial review to **clarify the legal status** of workers in the absence of legislation that has kept pace with rapidly changing working practices. In this instance, the Employment Rights Act (1996) and Working Time Regulations (1998) were both enacted more than two decades ago and prior to the significant rise in flexible working within the so-called 'gig' economy.

Box 8.3   Case study 2: setting legal precedents

An NHS Trust v *Y* (2018)

In July 2018 the Supreme Court ruled that legal permission was no longer needed to withdraw treatment from patients in a permanent vegetative state. For more than 20 years, doctors have been required to seek approval of a court, usually the Court of Protection, in a process that can take months or years, and it costs health authorities about £50,000 in legal fees to lodge an appeal, even when relatives agree that withdrawal of treatment would be in the best interests of the patient.

The Supreme Court's ruling **changes established legal practice** in making clear that courts need not be involved in these sorts of cases, so long as doctors and families agree that withdrawal is in the best interests of the patient.

However, the judgement is a highly controversial one, dividing opinion and cutting across religious, moral and ethical beliefs. For supporters of the ruling, it removes an unnecessary bureaucratic obstacle at what is often a tragic time. For opponents, the ruling removes a vital legal safeguard for a small but extremely vulnerable group of people.

Box 8.4   Case study 3: reviewing the legality of parliamentary legislature

Steinfield and Keidan v *Secretary of State for International Development* (2018)

Under the Civil Partnership Act 2004, only two people of the same sex may enter into a civil partnership. The Marriage (Same Sex couples) Act 2013 (MSSCA) made marriage of same-sex couples lawful. However, the CPA was not repealed when the MSSCA was enacted, meaning that whilst same-sex couples have a choice as to whether to enter into a civil partnership or to marry, different-sex couples do not.

In June 2018, the Supreme Court overruled a Court of Appeal decision, to rule instead that the Civil Partnership Act 2004 is **'incompatible' with the European Convention on Human Rights** as it applies only to same-sex couples and therefore amounted to discrimination. The case saw the Supreme Court use its power of judicial review to place significant pressure on the government to change the law and allow heterosexual couples to become civil partners. On 2 October 2018, Prime Minister Theresa May announced that the government would support legislation to guarantee the same rights for mixed-sex couples in civil partnerships.

> **Box 8.5** **Case study 4: determining whether public bodies have acted *ultra vires***
>
> **The UK withdrawal from the EU (Scotland) Bill — a reference by the Attorney General and the Advocate General for Scotland (2018)**
>
> The UK Supreme Court was asked to rule on whether the EU exit bill passed by the Scottish Parliament in March 2018 was constitutional and 'properly within devolved legislative powers'. As the UK government's Brexit negotiations continued, the Scottish Parliament had sought to affirm its own rights, in formerly EU-regulated areas such as agriculture and fisheries, for when powers returned to the UK from the EU.
>
> In April 2018, the UK government's law officers, the Attorney General and the Advocate General for Scotland, referred the Scottish legislation to the Supreme Court. At the hearing in July 2018, Lord Keen, the Advocate General for Scotland, told judges that the legislation passed by Members of the Scottish Parliament (MSPs) in March was outside the competence of the Scottish Parliament.
>
> By late November 2018 the Supreme Court had still not reached a verdict. Visit the Supreme Court's website **www.supremecourt.org** for the latest information.

Have recent events demonstrated that the power and influence of the Supreme Court is growing?

Yes

Several factors have elevated the significance of the Supreme Court and the consequences of its rulings in recent years. There is little doubt that the growth in scope and scale of EU law and also the responsibility that judges have to make 'declarations of incompatibility' where parliamentary statutes conflict with the Human Rights Act have had the most bearing on Court power. These two elements have progressively drawn judges into the political arena seen most starkly by the rise in the number of rulings from its first full year of the Court in 2010 to 2018 (see Table 8.2).

Politicisation is the process by which individuals traditionally regarded as being above or beyond the party-political fray are drawn into it. In 2018 alone, the Supreme Court ruled on cases that some regard as the domain of special interests, such as on gay marriage, euthanasia, marital and parental rights and abortion, and ruled against the Ministry of Justice, the Metropolitan Police and Her Majesty's Revenue and Customs (HMRC). Whilst the growing level of 'independence' and challenge to the political establishment in defence of civil liberties is welcomed by many, others have less support for the activities of an unelected and unrepresentative body in this sphere.

Table 8.2 Number of Supreme Court rulings, 2010–18

Year	Number of Supreme Court rulings
2010	56
2011	79
2012	84
2013	98
2014	90
2015	83
2016	75
2017	109
2018 (to November)	66

Source: www.supremecourt.org/decidedcases

No

It is important to note that because the UK does not have a codified constitution, despite perceptions of growing Court power, it remains impossible for the Supreme Court to 'strike down' Acts of Parliament or thwart the will of the government in the same way that the US Supreme Court can declare invalid Acts of Congress and force the president to back down.

The UK's departure from the European Union will inevitably have an impact on the status and power of the Supreme Court. Withdrawing from the Treaty of Rome will mean that EU law will no longer take precedence over UK law. This will have the twin effects of removing a significant element of the Court's caseload and also removing a court (the European Court of Justice) from its position of superiority over UK law. That said, many critics of the UK's perceived 'rights culture' conflate the European Convention on Human Rights (ECHR) with the European Union. In reality, leaving the EU will not remove the UK's obligations under the ECHR as the two are entirely separate.

For many long-standing commentators, the key cases that the Supreme Court has decided — in 2018 and previously — do not represent a significant departure from those decided by the Law Lords prior to the Court's creation in 2009. The prediction by the first Court president, Lord Phillips, that the creation of the Supreme Court would be a change of 'form rather than substance' appears to have been largely borne out.

Comparison: UK and US Supreme Courts

For students studying comparative politics, there is a requirement to compare and debate the UK and US Supreme Courts and their resulting impact on politics and government, their relative powers, levels of independence and their effectiveness in protecting rights. There are a number of important areas of comparison and contrast when it comes to judges and courts in the UK and USA.

■ The codified US constitution provides for far greater political significance where US judges are concerned. US Supreme Court justices are referred to as the 'guardians of the Constitution', as they frequently use their power of judicial review to clarify the meaning of the 230-year-old US Constitution in modern America. This means that responsibilities set out in the Constitution, such as the powers of the presidency, Congress and federal governments, are effectively determined by the US Supreme Court. The absence of a codified constitution in the UK means that the Court in the UK is seen largely as a legal body, rather than a political one.

■ Nominations of Supreme Court justices in the USA are made by the president and confirmed by the Senate. The ideological balance of the Court is therefore affected by the ideological stance of the nominating president. The security of tenure enjoyed by justice in the USA means that presidential influence can last many years.

Edexcel	Comparative Politics 6.2.7	Comparing aspects of UK and US Supreme Courts and their resulting impact on politics and government; the relative extent of their powers and their levels of independence
AQA	3.2.2.3	The similarities and differences of Supreme Courts; their impact on government and politics and the relative extent of their powers. A comparison of the relative independence of the judiciary in the UK and the USA

Both specifications require knowledge and understanding of the extent to which rational, cultural and structural approaches can be used to account for these similarities and differences.

Summary

This chapter has dealt primarily with developments in the senior judiciary in 2018 — the changes to the composition of the Supreme Court that took place and the ongoing debate about the nature and scope of Court power. Students also require significant knowledge of how the three institutions of state — judiciary, executive and parliament — interact in the creation and the administration of the law, and further debates include:

■ the extent to which the principle of the rule of law guides legislative and judicial activity
■ the 'law-making' powers of judges as they set legal precedents through their interpretation of common law

- the preservation of judicial independence, and the nature and composition of the senior judiciary in preserving judicial neutrality
- the conflict that exists between the upholding of civil liberties and the enhanced protection of the public
- perceptions of the growing power of judges, in conflict with democratically elected governments

Further reading and research

- Read 'Has the UK Supreme Court changed anything?', Katie Shapiro, *Politics Review*, September 2018.
- Go to **www.judiciary.uk** and look up the summary of judicial diversity in the Judicial Diversity Statistics 2018.
- View the *Guardian*'s Supreme Court page for up-to-date analysis on cases and decisions (**www.theguardian.com/law/uk-supreme-court**).
- Visit the Supreme Court's website for an understanding of the role of the Court and details on decided cases (**www.supremecourt.uk**).

Chapter 9

Devolution: developments in the devolved assemblies in 2018

Exam success

The examination specifications focus on the both the role and the power of devolved assemblies in the UK, and the resulting impact that this has on the field of UK politics. The best candidates will understand that there is no uniform impact created by the devolved assembly. Rather, each of the bodies in Northern Ireland, Wales and Scotland has quite different impacts on its region and on the UK more generally. Top answers will recognise the importance of unique examples from 2018, including Northern Ireland unofficially breaking the record for the longest time without a government in an era of peace. They will also be able to evaluate the impact of the Wales Act of 2014 and 2017, both of which came into force in some guise in 2018.

Edexcel	UK Government 1.3	The role and powers of devolved bodies in the UK and the impact of this devolution on the UK.
AQA	3.1.1.5	The roles, powers and responsibilities of the different devolved bodies in the UK

Context

Devolution in the UK is asymmetric — it lacks uniformity between the devolved bodies of the UK. Devolution was promised as part of Labour's manifesto 1997 for Scotland and Wales and an ensuing referendum ensured that there actually was support for devolution, in contrast to the 1979 referenda. The passage of the Scotland Act and the Government of Wales Act in 1998 allowed for the creation of the Scottish Parliament at Holyrood and the National Assembly for Wales at the Senedd. Northern Ireland had previously had devolved powers but these had been abolished under the 1973 Northern Ireland Constitution Act and direct rule instituted from Westminster in response to 'the Troubles'. The Good Friday Agreement, which brokered peace in Northern Ireland and established a new Northern Irish Parliament at Stormont, was agreed to in a referendum of 1998.

The resulting settlement saw each devolved body having different legislative and fiscal powers over its region. For example, whilst Scotland was given primary legislative powers, Wales only got secondary legislative powers, leaving it more dependent on Westminster to pass laws. In the years following the initial settlement, laws have been passed to enlarge and to some extent equalise the powers of the devolved bodies, although absolute parity has not yet been achieved.

As with almost every area of UK politics in 2018, the Brexit bill played a huge role in this area, with Scotland's First Minister Nicolas Sturgeon claiming that it ripped up the devolution settlement of the UK. In Wales, debates and draft legislation continued to look at the renaming of the Welsh Assembly, whilst the Wales Act of 2017 came into force on the 1 April 2018. In Northern Ireland, following a row over a botched energy scheme, the Assembly has been without an executive since January 2017.

Wales in 2018

The Wales Act of 2017 came into force in 2018, giving Wales powers more akin to those given to the Scottish Parliament. The Welsh Secretary claimed: '... today is when the National Assembly becomes a full law-making parliament.' The most significant of these changes was the introduction of a 'reserved matters' model for the Welsh Assembly. This meant that rather than having an Act of Parliament which listed the powers that Wales was given (the 'conferred powers' model), the new Act instead listed those powers that were reserved to Westminster. Therefore, if something is not deemed to be 'reserved', it is automatically given to law-makers in the Welsh Assembly.

The Act was not universally welcomed. Whilst it gave power to Wales in some areas, it seemed to 'roll back' its power in others. For example, the Human Transplantation Act of 2013, which made organ donation opt-out rather than opt-in, would now require approval from Westminster.

Box 9.1 **The Welsh Secretary Alun Cairns comments on the implementation of the Wales Act 2017**

Today is when the Assembly not only becomes a full law-making parliament but also the day they inherit and accept powers on a much wider basis.

These powers come from energy to transport to highways to road signs so the Assembly can decide on its policies in a whole host of areas including taxation.

Some taxes will have been devolved and will come into effect very soon*, but also as a result of this Act the Welsh government will have responsibility for raising its own money through income tax. Now of course I want to see that income tax rate cut but that's a matter for the Assembly to justify their decisions and spending.

*In addition to the 2018 power, from September 2019 Wales can set teachers' pay and can vary income tax from April 2019, although not change income tax bands as Scotland can.

Also in 2018, the first Welsh taxes in over 800 years came into force. This was a result of the Wales Act 2014, which transferred the power over Stamp Duty and Landfill Tax to the Welsh Assembly. On the 1 April 2018, Wales introduced two new taxes:

- **The Land Transactions Tax:** a Welsh tax replacing the UK Stamp-Duty Tax. People buying propertied valued at under £150,000 would be exempt from this tax, rather than under £125,000 as under the UK tax. However, properties valued at over £400,000 would be subject to a higher tax, at 7.5% rather than 5%.

- **The Landfill Disposals Tax:** this was a tax on waste being sent to landfill and charged by weight. Unlike the tax above, this was deliberately set at a level similar to that in England to avoid waste tourism.

It was estimated that these two new taxes would raise £1 billion for Wales over the first 4 years of their use.

> ### Box 9.2   Comments from Mark Drakeford, finance secretary for Wales
>
> From April, Wales will introduce the first Welsh taxes in almost 800 years, supporting first-time buyers and boosting business.
>
> The devolution of tax powers provides us with the opportunity to reshape and make changes to improve existing taxes to better meet Wales' needs and priorities. I have always been clear that we will use these powers to help improve fairness and support jobs and economic growth in Wales.
>
> These new progressive rates and bands for land transaction tax and landfill disposals tax will make a real difference to people's lives; help change behaviours and deliver improvements to communities across Wales. We are being bold but balanced and leading the way in creating a fair and progressive tax system.

What's in a name?

In July 2018, the National Assembly for Wales Commission published its proposed reforms for the Welsh Assembly. It formally proposed changing the name of the devolved body to the Welsh Parliament and lowering the voting age for the body to 16-year-olds.

The name change caused some disquiet amongst members of the Welsh Assembly, currently known as AMs (assembly members). They would become instead MWPs (members of the Welsh Parliament), which raised concern this would colloquially become 'muppets', as the Welsh 'w' is pronounced in a manner similar to 'u'. However, it was felt after consultation that this name change was more befitting of the constitutional status of the devolved body.

The proposed reforms also included increasing the size of the Assembly and reviewing the electoral system used to elect its members. All of these proposed reforms were consequences of powers gained in the 2017 Act, and while they have yet to be passed through the Welsh Assembly, the plans are that they will be in time for the next election in 2021.

Northern Ireland in 2018

The Northern Irish Assembly has been suspended since January 2017. However, after months of wrangling, talks to try to bring about the reopening of Stormont collapsed in February 2018. Whilst the initial problems arose about an energy scheme, they have since grown to include divisive issues such as an Irish language bill, measures regarding investigations into 'the Troubles' and same-sex marriage.

The Northern Irish secretary took the decision in September 2018 to reduce the salaries of the members of the Assembly by £13,000 given that they were not fulfilling all of the functions of an elected representative.

The result of this suspension has not only been no formal government in Northern Ireland since January 2017, but has also led to significant questions over who is running the country. In the absence of elected politicians, civil servants had been administering the country's processes. However, a High Court ruling in May 2018 threw this into disarray. The High Court ruled that an incinerator approved by a senior civil servant could not go ahead as the decision should have been taken by a minister.

The judge in the case commented that the suspension of Stormont could not have meant that 'such decision-making would continue in Northern Ireland in the absence of ministers without the protection of democratic accountability'. Before this, the Northern Ireland Office at Westminster had been reluctant to intervene, or to impose direct rule, for fears it may have made the stalemate in Stormont even harder to overcome. After this decision however, it became necessary for the Northern Ireland secretary to look for remedies to this problem. In September therefore, the Northern Ireland Office announced a plan to allow civil servants to exercise a similar power to that which they had before this ruling.

Issues surrounding 'the Troubles' in Northern Ireland – the often violent conflict in the 1960s and 1970s between unionists and republicans – were also an issue in 2018. The UK government launched a public consultation to address the legacy of this violence. This hugely controversial topic saw the deadline for public input extended by a month to 5 October to allow more people to have their say. The UK government hoped the outcome would enable Northern Ireland to look to a more peaceful future.

Of course, Brexit has also proved especially relevant to Northern Ireland given the prospect of a 'hard border' between Northern Ireland and the Republic of Ireland. However, Theresa May caused controversy in her plans to avoid a 'hard border'. Should there be no other solution, Northern Ireland would effectively be allowed to remain in the single market to avoid the necessity for such a border, but May said that the Northern Irish Assembly would have to vote to agree on this before it could come into effect, essentially giving it a veto. This suggestion of September 2018 was especially controversial given the lack of a government at Stormont for 20 months at that point.

Not a record-breaking suspension
The suspension of Stormont meant that, at the end of August, Northern Ireland could have become country that has had the longest time without a government during peacetime. It could have beaten the previous record by Belgium set at 541 days without a government in 2010–11. However, Guinness World Records said that Northern Ireland was not eligible for the record as during their suspension, laws could still be made for its country from Westminster.

The impact of devolution

The contrasting examples of Wales and Northern Ireland provide an interesting insight into the impact of devolution. With Wales becoming more responsible for its own taxes and finances and moving to a 'reserved model' of powers, sovereignty seems to be devolving further from Parliament. Indeed, the Plaid Cymru 2017 manifesto commented: '... it remains our ambition for Wales to become an independent nation, standing on its own two feet.' This is especially notable now that Wales has far greater control over the size and nature of the national assembly. Nonetheless, the further devolution over power to Wales over the past decade does appear to have dampened enthusiasm for independence, with polls supporting it being 10% lower in 2018 than in 2011, which seems to suggest that the settlement as it stands is broadly accepted. Whilst the new Act did give Wales some more powers, it also took some away, and it would no longer be able to make laws that it has made previously without the consent of Westminster. This highlights the fluid and evolutionary nature of devolution in the UK.

The situation in Northern Ireland further underlines the flexibility of devolution. The statutory impact seems to be a gentle flow of increasing power to the devolved assemblies. The reality, however, is more fraught, especially in the light of Brexit, which has so many consequences for the UK and devolved regions. The lack of a government at Stormont, and the attempts by the UK cabinet secretary for Northern Ireland demonstrates the important role Westminster still plays in devolved regions.

Comparison: devolution in the UK and federalism in the US

The systems of devolution and federalism have a similar appearance. However, the way in which they function, and the reasons for this, are quite different. Obviously, the size difference between the USA and UK is vast, but where arguments have become more common about further devolution in the UK, the federal (national) government seems to grow ever bigger in the USA.

- The system of federalism in the USA is far more uniform than devolution in the UK. Whilst different states have different laws, they have the same law-making powers over the same areas. Therefore, it becomes a choice of each state to make laws that suit their citizens and culture. The devolved regions of the UK can end up with different laws not because they want to, but because they have been given different powers.
- Both devolution and federalism have allowed regions of the two countries to trial new policies. Whilst Scotland has free university tuition for Scottish citizens, and Wales has an opt-out rather than opt-in organ donation policy, states in the US have used their powers to create unique laws. Maine, for example, had universal healthcare long before Obamacare, and Oregon allows for euthanasia under certain circumstances.
- The basis of federalism and devolution is entirely different. The states are guaranteed their power by the US Constitution, whilst the devolved bodies were given their power by Parliament. This has meant that states in the USA may be

more willing to defy national government, for example by legalising marijuana and refusing to enforce national immigration policies, whilst the devolved bodies are very much still under the control of Westminster as highlighted by Brexit and its planned imposition on Scotland.

Edexcel	Comparative Politics 6.2.1	The similarities and differences between the US federal system and the UK system of devolution
AQA	3.2.2.1	Similarities and differences between the devolution model in the UK and the federal model in the USA

Summary

As Welsh politician Ron Davies said: 'Devolution is a process not an event.' And so it seems to continue to be. The development of Welsh powers in 2018 show the continuous development of devolution as a process and the slow 'churn' of more powers drifting to the regions. Even in the case of Northern Ireland, the unwillingness of Westminster to simply take control of Stormont underlines the importance that self-government is seen to hold. However, devolution is not without issues.

Further debates include:

- whether it is time to seriously consider the creation of an English Parliament
- whether it is necessary to review the asymmetric nature of devolution in the UK, and try to achieve uniformity
- the necessity of exploring devolution to regions within England
- the effectiveness of English votes for English laws in creating some form of 'devolution' for England alone
- the role and significance of Brexit, given the rejection of the Westminster bill and the creation of Brexit bills by devolved assemblies themselves.

Further reading and research

- Read 'Powerhouse parliaments: is Holyrood the world's most devolved?', 16 May 2016, www.bbc.co.uk to identify the key differences in the asymmetric devolution in the UK.
- Read Stephen Crabb's article 'Here are five Assembly laws which would have required UK government consent under the Wales Office's plans', 15 November 2015 (www.walesonline.co.uk) to find out more about the laws that Wales could no longer have made under its new powers. Has Wales become more or less powerful?
- Find out more about the impact of Brexit on devolution by reading 'Reality check: has the UK's devolution settlement been ripped up?', Stuart Nicolson, 14 June 2018, www.bbc.co.uk.
- Aiming for an A? Compare the theory of English votes for English laws (EVEL) to the reality as demonstrated by Project EVEL. Has it achieved its goals?
  - 'English votes: A beginner's guide', 22 October 2015, www.bbc.co.uk
  - http://evel.uk/data

Chapter 10

Brexit: developments in 2018

Exam success

This chapter pulls together a wide range of theoretical topics on the Politics specifications as the issue of Brexit cuts across so many of these topics. For the best candidates, some of the issues posed by Brexit have been the continually shifting political landscape it has created coupled with the difficulty of divorcing publically inflammatory headlines from politically useful ones. Top answers will draw on the example of Brexit in a specific and well-understood manner, explicitly demonstrating the links between this and the topic at hand. They will see the issues surrounding Brexit as individual and unique, and will draw on detailed information rather than just referencing 'Brexit' as an event alone. As the leaving date of March 2019 approaches, there will doubtless be further changes and developments, all of which a top candidate will continue to monitor.

Context

The dissolution of Parliament in 1628 by Charles I was accompanied by his declaration that 'princes are not bound to give an account of their actions but to God alone'. The result of the 2016 Brexit referendum has posed this same problem in twenty-first-century politics — namely, where exactly does power lie in the UK political system? Amongst those trying to exercise power, there has been popular sovereignty exercised through referendums, government decisions from the consent granted by representative democracy, parliamentary sovereignty as granted through the UK constitution and judicial power through the act of judicial review. Then there is the power beyond central government — the devolved bodies, the EU and the media, all trying to influence the outcome of the Brexit negotiations. With all of these conflicting interests, Brexit is a seminal example of how British politics works... or sometimes, does not.

Where does power lie?

Pressure groups

Edexcel	UK Politics 1.3	Pressure groups and other influences
AQA	3.1.2.4	Pressure groups

In 2018, the Vote Leave campaign was fined £61,000 by the Electoral Commission for breaking electoral laws.

The People's Vote and the *Independent* launched e-petitions for a second referendum gaining over 300,000 and over a million votes respectively and organised a 'March for the Future' in London on 20 October. Over 700,000 attended this protest, the biggest since Stop the War in 2003.

The controversy over Brexit has also reignited the issue of Scottish independence; as a nation, the Scottish voted in a majority to remain in the EU. A pro-independence pressure group All Under One Banner organised a protest march in Edinburgh in October which saw tens of thousands of people take to the streets demanding a referendum before the end of the Brexit transition period in 2021.

Political parties

Edexcel	UK Politics 2	Political parties
AQA	3.1.2.3	Political parties

Factions within the Conservative Party emerged strongly over Theresa May's Chequers plan. Conservative MPs supported three different outcomes – a potential no-deal Brexit (supported by Rees-Mogg), some form of Brexit deal (supported by Boles), or a second referendum (supported by Wollaston).

Factions within the Labour Party emerged too, initially due to the lack of a distinct policy over Brexit. At the 2018 conference, divisions were evident over support for a second referendum. Sir Keir Starmer has put forward six tests for any Brexit deal: 'If Theresa May brings back a deal that fails our tests – and that looks increasingly likely – Labour will vote against it. No ifs, no buts.' At the 2018 party conference, Corbyn pledged to support a 'sensible deal' that included a customs union and no hard border in Northern Ireland.

Box 10.1 Sir Keir Starmer's six tests for any Brexit deal

1 Does it ensure a strong and collaborative future relationship with the EU?
2 Does it deliver the 'exact same benefits' as we currently have as members of the single market and customs union?
3 Does it ensure fair management of migration in the interests of the economy and communities?
4 Does it defend rights and protections and prevent a race to the bottom?
5 Does it protect national security and our capacity to tackle cross-border crime?
6 Does it deliver for all regions and nations of the UK?

Nationalist parties Plaid Cymru and the SNP both launched their own Brexit legislation, fearful of the impact that Brexit would have on their countries. The SNP also suggested that their support for a second referendum on Brexit could be tied to a second referendum on Scottish independence.

Elections and referendums

Edexcel	UK Politics 3.2	Referendums and how they are used
AQA	3.1.2.2	Elections and referendums

Obviously the Brexit referendum itself is a useful example for the referendum topic, as is the closeness of the result which has raised questions over legitimacy and highlighted the concerns of referendums creating 'tyranny of the majority'. However, the arguments surrounding a second referendum in 2018 plus the reignited issue of a second independence referendum for Scotland also demonstrates the increasing acceptance and expectation of referendums in the UK as a form of popular and direct democracy.

Voting behaviour and media

Edexcel	UK Politics 4	Voting behaviour and the media
AQA	3.1.2.2	Elections and referendums

The EU Commissioner called for the UK media to be more responsible for its reporting over Brexit after *The Sun* headline 'EU dirty rats'. She called for less divisive reporting and an expectation that the media should not encourage hate. Such division has been seen through Brexit headlines such as the *Daily Mail*'s 'Enemies of the people' (UK judges) and the *Telegraph*'s 'Mutineers' (remain-leaning Conservatives).

The UK constitution

Edexcel	UK Government 1	The constitution
AQA	3.1.1.1	The nature and sources of the British constitution

Brexit represents a huge change to the UK constitution and demonstrates its relative flexibility. Professor Bogdanor wrote: '...we are moving from a codified and protected constitutional system to an uncodified and unprotected one based on the sovereignty of Parliament. We are also moving from a system in which our rights have been enlarged to one where some of our rights will in effect have been abolished, as a result of a deliberate decision on the part of the government.'

Parliament

Edexcel	UK Government 2	Parliament
AQA	3.1.1.2	The structure and role of Parliament

The role of Parliament in Brexit has been extensive:

- The Lords defeated the government on 18 different occasions in 2018 over issues to do with Brexit.
- One of the Lords proposed amendments was that the Commons should have the opportunity to block a 'no deal' Brexit. However, in a victory for the government, a vote in June 2018 rejected this amendment 319–303, with just

four Labour MPs voting against the amendment and six Conservative MPs voting for it, along with the Liberal Democrats and the SNP.

- On one day alone in June, the House of Commons voted for the government and against the House of Lords in 19 proposed amendments to the EU withdrawal bill.
- The opposition used the archaic humble address to try to force the release of government Brexit documents.
- Three different opposition days (led by Labour, the SNP and Plaid Cymru) raised issues to do with Brexit.
- The EU withdrawal bill was amended in December 2017.
- Brexit Secretary Dominic Raab suggested the 'meaningful vote' in Parliament would be between whatever deal May offers and no deal. This caused huge controversy over the role of Parliament in the Brexit deal, with Sir Keir Starmer responding: 'That is not a meaningful vote and Ministers can't be allowed to silence Parliament.' Valerie Vaz described it as 'the most outrageous power grab' that would take sovereignty away from Parliament.

Prime minister and the executive

Edexcel	UK Government 3	Prime Minister and Executive
AQA	3.1.1.3	The Prime Minister and cabinet

The negotiations with the EU over Brexit go some way to demonstrate the power of the prime minister. Theresa May claimed in June 2018 that 'Parliament cannot tie the hands of government in negotiations'.

May's negotiations with the EU over Brexit created tension, with the President of the European Commission commenting: 'If you leave the union, you are of course no longer part of our single market, and certainly not only in the parts of it you choose.' Such was the impasse over the negotiations that the EU proposed extending the post-Brexit transition by 'a few months' if it was necessary. This might allow for a better Brexit outcome, but it does serve to highlight the inability of May to secure a broadly agreeable Brexit deal.

May lost cabinet ministers over the issue of Brexit (Johnson, Davis) and had to deal with cabinet divisions between the Brexiteers and remainers with Mourdant and McVey also hinting at possible resignations.

Jeremy Corbyn removed Owen Smith from the shadow cabinet role of Northern Ireland secretary after he supported a second referendum. Smith claimed that in order to honour the Good Friday Agreement in Northern Ireland, the UK needed to remain in the customs union and the single market.

The Supreme Court

Edexcel	UK Government 4.1	The Supreme Court and its interactions with, and influence over, the legislative and policy-making processes.
AQA	3.1.1.4	The judiciary

Although decided in 2017, the Supreme Court ruling in *R (Miller)* v *Secretary of State for Exiting the European Union* continued to have ramifications in 2018. The case ruled that Article 50, the trigger to leave the EU, could not be done by the government but had to be done by Parliament, underpinning parliamentary sovereignty. The importance of this action helps to support parliamentary calls for a meaningful vote on the final deal due to its sovereignty.

In July 2018, Scotland went to the Supreme Court over Brexit. The Scottish government claimed the EU withdrawal bill amounted to a 'power grab' by UK Parliament. They therefore drew up and passed their own withdrawal legislation but this was challenged in the Court by the UK government which sought clarity over whether such an action was within the devolved powers of Scotland. The Supreme Court heard the case, being told the Scottish bill was 'perfectly practical'. By November 2018 the Supreme Court had still not reached a verdict.

Other courts have also been involved in the issue of Brexit. In the High Court in 2018, a challenge to the legality of Brexit at all was rejected by judges.

Devolution

Edexcel	UK Government 1.3	The role and powers of devolved bodies in the UK, and the impact of this devolution on the UK
AQA	3.1.1.5	Devolution

Scotland

In Scotland, the issue of Brexit proved highly contentious. The EU withdrawal bill proposed by Parliament would put all EU legislation onto the UK statute books and then Parliament could decide what to repeal. However, this caused concern in Holyrood as many of the issues in EU law directly affected Scotland; the Scottish Parliament claimed that by putting them into UK law with the possibility that Parliament might repeal them, and with Parliament wanting a final say on how these laws would now operate, the Scottish Parliament could effectively lose power. This led to the Scottish withdrawal bill being produced, referred to as 'the continuity bill'. This bill would bring the relevant EU laws across onto the Scottish statute books, allowing the Scottish Parliament to amend or repeal them. Questions over whether Scotland had the power to do this ended up in the UK Supreme Court.

Wales

A similar concern was exercised in Wales and a continuity bill was also produced. The Welsh Assembly and the UK government managed to reach an agreement over this in April 2018, but with Wales' finance secretary Mark Drakeford saying the agreement would ensure that the powers 'currently devolved remain devolved'. The reaction from the Welsh nationalist party Plaid Cymru was less supportive. Leader Leanne Wood said: 'By capitulating to Westminster on the EU Withdrawal Bill, the Labour government is selling Wales down the river. This is a bare-faced Westminster power grab which undermines the will of the people of Wales who voted for more powers in two referendums.'

Northern Ireland

In Northern Ireland, Brexit was particularly contentious. With the Republic of Ireland being in the EU, and Northern Ireland leaving as part of the UK, an issue arose over how the border between these two countries would work. Both the UK and EU agree this should not be a hard border – this means there should not be a physical border with checks on those passing through it. The EU proposed that Northern Ireland could be treated differently to the rest of the UK, but Theresa May rejected any plan where Northern Ireland would have different regulations to the rest of the UK. In case of no Brexit deal being negotiated, it became necessary to plan a 'backstop' – a plan for Northern Ireland under these circumstances. Following the negotiations of October 2018, there was no agreement on either the backstop or the final agreement. For almost the entire time since the Brexit referendum, Northern Ireland has been without a government, which has also hampered its input on the border negotiations. (See Chapter 9 on devolution for other problems created by Brexit in Northern Ireland.)

The European Union

Edexcel	UK Government 4.3	The aims, role and impact of the European Union (EU) on UK government
AQA	3.1.2.5	The European Union

Given that Brexit is all about leaving the EU, it will completely alter the UK relationship with the EU and its institutions. As can be seen in the Chequers plan however, and through the suggestions of different types of deals that might be possible, there will not be a complete severing of ties, but what the future relationship will be remains to be seen.

Negotiations in October 2018

The Brexit negotiations that took place in October were nicknamed the 'moment of truth' by European Council President Donald Tusk: 'Everybody shared the view that while there are positive elements in the Chequers proposal, the suggested framework for economic cooperation will not work, not least because it risks undermining the single market. The moment of truth for Brexit negotiations will be the October European Council. In October we expect maximum progress and results in the Brexit talks.'

What is the Chequers plan?

The Chequers plan, named after the prime ministers' country residence at which it was agreed, covered four key areas – the economy, security, future areas of cooperation and the needed frameworks to enforce the agreement. It recognised that the freedom of movement would be ended, and a new framework for movement between the EU and UK would need to be established. It proposed:

- **A common rulebook for all goods:** a UK–EU free trade area with common rules for industrial and agricultural goods. This would include that a treaty committing to 'continued harmonisation' with EU rules should ensure there is no hard border in Northern Ireland. Parliament would be allowed to choose to accept or reject future EU rules, recognising the consequences that might have and recognising that the UK and EU will not have the same access to each other's markets as they currently have.
- **Commitment to open and fair trade:** establishing cooperative arrangements on competition and maintaining high standards for the environment, climate change, social and employment and consumer protection.
- **A joint framework:** the rules would be interpreted by UK courts in the UK and EU courts in the EU. The framework would include the methods by which disputes can be resolved.
- **A facilitated customs arrangement:** removing the need for customs checks between the EU and the UK, with the UK able to apply tariffs to the rest of the world.

Table 10.1 The advantages and disadvantages of the Chequers plan

Advantages	Disadvantages
It ensures there is no hard border in Northern Ireland.	It is not a complete break with the EU, and pleases neither Brexiteers nor remainers.
It allows free trade with the EU without customs checks.	The collections of tariffs would be very complex.
It fulfils the referendum promise of Brexit.	It still requires a great deal of cooperation with the EU on policy issues.

What happened at the 'moment of truth' negotiations?

These Brexit negotiations took place on what was once supposed to be the date for a final deal to give both sides time to ratify it. This was not forthcoming. So what did happen?

- No Brexit deal was struck predominantly due to the issue of how to prevent a hard border in Northern Ireland, which both sides agree is a necessity.
- The result of there being no deal reached was an offer from the EU to extend the transition period by 'a few months'.
- Criticism of Theresa May was ever present, with David Davis encouraging ministers to rebel against any Brexit deal under the Chequers plan. Such criticism could result in Parliament rejecting any deal that May manages to broker.

- The plans for a summit in November were scrapped given the lack of progress, and moved to December at the earliest. This further limited the time that Parliament and the EU would have to approve any final deal.

Why is Brexit so difficult to negotiate?

One of the main problems in negotiating Brexit is that the referendum did not settle what type of Brexit was wanted. For politicians such as Rees-Mogg or Johnson, Brexit is an opportunity to sever ties with the EU and for the UK to forge its own trade deals. For others, a 'softer' Brexit is preferable, with the UK remaining in a customs union and reaping at least some of the benefits that EU membership offers.

Furthermore, having held a referendum, it is difficult for either the government or Parliament not to deliver some form of Brexit. Therefore, with backing out not being a very realistic option, the decision over what type of Brexit is achieved is even more important, and yet ideologically there is no consensus within either major party, let alone between them.

Comparison: the importance of national events in the UK and the USA

The nature of politics in both the UK and the US can be affected by national events that occur beyond the control of the governments. This might be natural disasters, economic events, terrorist attacks or events such as Brexit. National events tend to concentrate power in the executive as the representative of a nation. However, if public opinion begins to decline, the legislatures of both countries become more willing to scrutinise and challenge the executive branch.

Edexcel	Comparative Politics 6	Comparative approaches
AQA	3.2.2	Comparative politics

Summary

Even after March 2019, the issue of Brexit is unlikely to be settled. The extent of the controversy and the complexity of the negotiations are such that how Brexit will work remains to be seen, including whether a deal can even be reached.

Further debates include:

- whether the role of the Supreme Court can be justified without becoming inherently political
- whether it is necessary to reevaluate the use of referendums after the consequences of the Brexit referendum
- the necessity of Lords reform in order to strengthen its power
- the effectiveness of UK parties at presenting coherent alternative policies
- the role and significance of the media in shaping public opinion, and the expected responsibility of this role

Further reading and research

- Keep your knowledge current by going to **www.bbc.co.uk** and reading 'Brexit: All you need to know about the UK leaving the EU', Alex Hunt and Brian Wheeler (constantly updated).
- Read the report from the Electoral Commission 'Vote Leave fined and referred to the polic for breaking electoral law, 17 July 2018, **www.electoralcommission.org.uk**. Does this suggest referendums can never be fully legitimate?
- Find out more about the five Brexit scenarios published in August 2018 by reading 'Autumn surprises: possible scenarios for the next phase of Brexit', Jill Rutter and Joe Owen, **www.instituteforgovernment.org.uk**. Compare these to the deal that was struck.
- Aiming for an A? Read 'The mechanics of a further referendum on Brexit' by Jess Sargeant, Alan Renwick and Meg Russell on the UCL Constitution Unit's website (**www.ucl.ac.uk**). What does this suggest about the wider use of referendums in the UK?